IMO Workbook II

For Students of Grade 2 aspiring for Olympiads and other Competitive Examinations

Chandan Sukumar Senguta

Creative Commons Series

IMO Workbook II

For Students of Grade 2 aspiring for Olympiads and other Competitive Examinations

This Workbook is suitable for students of Grade II of National Curriculum. It will also provide some additional study materials for enhancing the involvement of the fellow student in daily practices of Mathematical operations. Some of the problems incorporated in this volume are from higher standards to link up the competency ladder in a suitable way. It is expected that fellow students enjoy all the worksheets and activity sheets thoroughly. Additional copy of such Worksheets can be used for the purpose of Evaluation.

One worksheet a day will be better than exhausting all the materials in a hurry. Some of the items can be used even for second and third time. Introduction of some familiar mathematical tools will make the success of this workbook more prominent. .it is expected that after passing through all the worksheets students deepen their understanding of place value of numbers and their understanding of and skill with addition, subtraction, multiplication, and division of whole numbers. Students may become competent to estimate, measure, and describe objects in space. They use different known and guided patterns to help solve problems. They represent number relationships and conduct simple comparative, sequence based and probability based experiments.

- o   mental addition and subtraction
- o   regrouping in addition and subtraction
- o   basic word problems
- o   multiplication tables and basic division facts
- o   Basic multiplication and related concepts
- o   Formation of division and multiplication sentences.
- o   clock to the minute and elapsed time calculations.
- o   basic money calculations (finding totals and change)
- o   place value and rounding with four-digit numbers
- o   quadrilaterals, perimeter, and area
- o   division and related concepts (remainder, word problems)
- o   measuring lines in inches and centimeters
- o   basic usage of measuring units

Contents

Model Paper I i

Model Paper II vii

Moodel Paper III ix

Activities xi

1. Worksheets.. 1

    Worksheet 1 1

    Worksheet 2 3

    Worksheet 3 5

    Worksheet 4 9

    Worksheet 5 12

    Worksheet 6 14

    Worksheet 7 15

    Worksheet 8 16

    Worksheet 9 19

    Worksheet 10 21

2. Daily Practice 23

    Worksheet 1 23

    Worksheet 2 27

    Worksheet 3 31

    Worksheet 4 32

    Worksheet 5 33

    Worksheet 6 35

    Worksheet 7 36

    Worksheet 8 38

    Worksheet 9 39

    Worksheet 10 41

    Worksheet 11 43

    Worksheet 12 45

    Worksheet 13 46

    Worksheet 14 47

CONTENTS

Worksheet 15 48

Worksheet 16 49

Worksheet 17 50

Sbject Enrichment 53

Achiever A..60

Achiever B..61

Achiever C..62

Achiever D 63

Achiever E 64

Achiever F 65

Achiever G 66

Achiever I..68

Achiever J..69

Achiever K...74

Achiever L 76

Achiever M 77

Achiever N 78

Achiever O 80

Achiever P...81

Achiever Q..82

Achiever R...84

Achiever S...89

Achiever T...90

Achiever U 91

Model Paper I

a Circle the number two thousand, five hundred sixteen:

     1,244 1,424 2,651 2,516 216

b. Circle the number one thousand, one:

     101   1,001 1,010 1,100 1,010

c. Circle the number nine thousand, four hundred:

     9,040 940   9,400 9,004 9,404

d. Write the following numbers in Standard Numeration:

1. three thousand, six hundred twenty-four ______________

2. six thousand, forty-three ______________

3. eight thousand, two ______________

e. Write the next counting number after 9,999: ______________

f. Write these numbers in ascending order,

     8,201 8,012 8,102 812   80,102

g. 6,934 =__thousands + __ones + __ tens + ____ hundreds

h. 8,256 = ______________ + ______________ + ________

i. 2,000 + ________ + 30 + 9 = 2,739;

j. 12,000 + ________ + 300 + 9 = 12,369;

k. Solve these problems:

591	1,283	3,215	300
+ 87	+ 6,074	− 2,806	− 27
-------	-----------	-----------	--------
-------	-----------	-----------	--------

I. 5 X 8 = 40 , then 50 X 400 = ____________ ;

j. Half of a dozen bananas = _________ bananas;

k. You put 606 marbles into different bags, ending up with the same number of marbles in each bag. How many marbles would be in each bag if there were 6 bags?_________

l. Represent the following fraction in fraction disc.

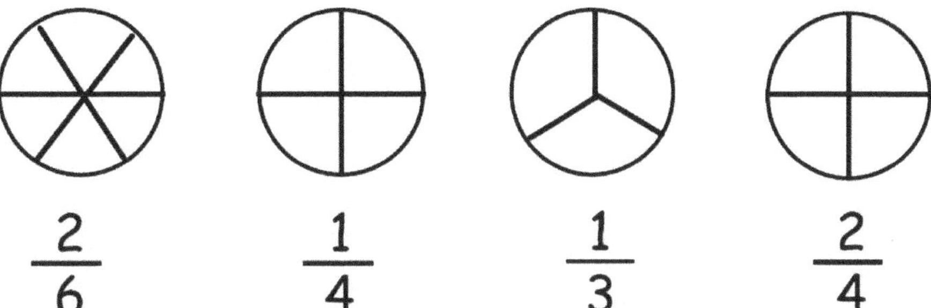

$$\frac{2}{6} \qquad \frac{1}{4} \qquad \frac{1}{3} \qquad \frac{2}{4}$$

m. Triangle of figure 1 has a right angle. Two sides of triangle 2 are equal to each other. All the three sides in triangle 3 are equal to each other.

Identify following triangles as Isosceles, Equilateral and Right Triangle.

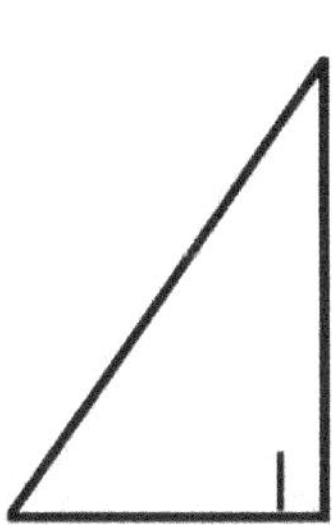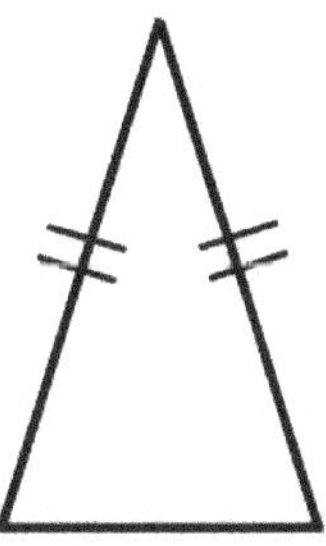

1. _________________   2. _________________   3. _________________

n. How many tens are there in 2,343?

o. Find the smallest two digit greatest number divisible by 2.

p. 2,000 + 46 tens + 4 tens + 21 tens + 35 ones = ______________ .

q. Identify the number pattern and write the missing numbers.

1. 3, _____ , 9, _____ , 15   2. 111, 115, _____, 123, 127

3. 50, 40, _____, 20,   4. 48, 46, _____, 42,

5. 98, 100, _____ , 104,   6. 7, _____ , 11, _____ , 15

7. 21, ____, ______, _____, ______, _______, _____, _____, 101

r. Identify the following shapes:

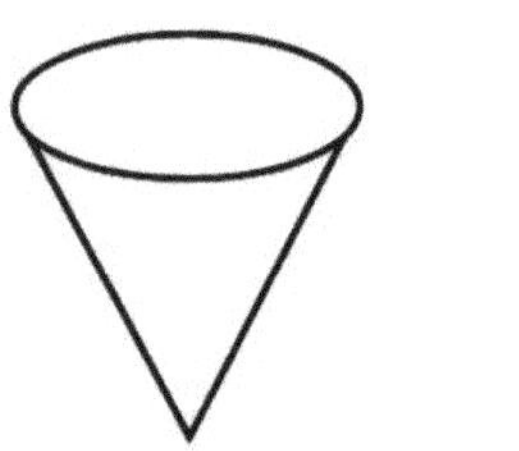 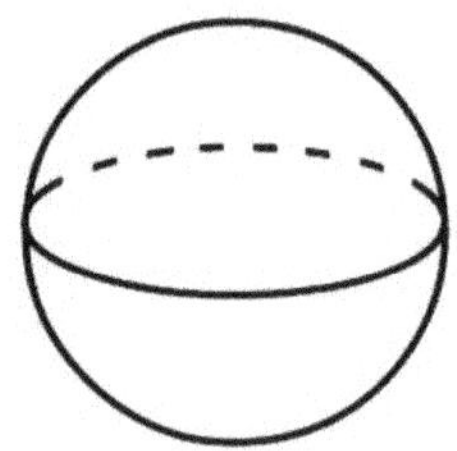 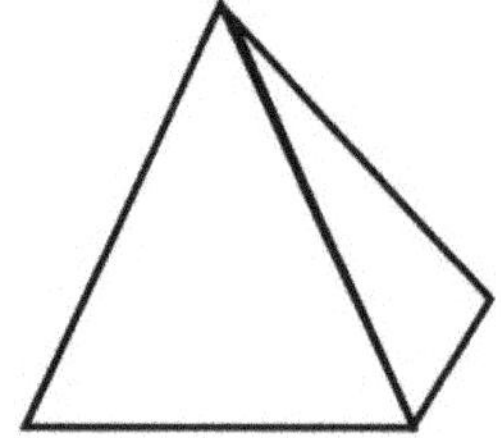 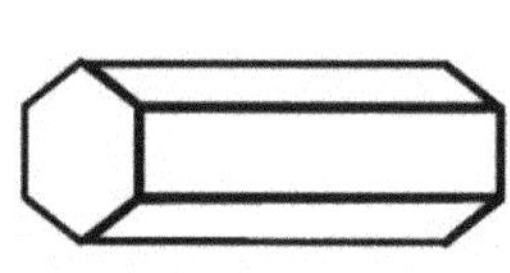

a.__________   b.__________   c.__________   d.__________

s. Select the numbers that round to 100.

A 38   B. 109   C. 162   D. 83   E. 93

t. Write the numbers:

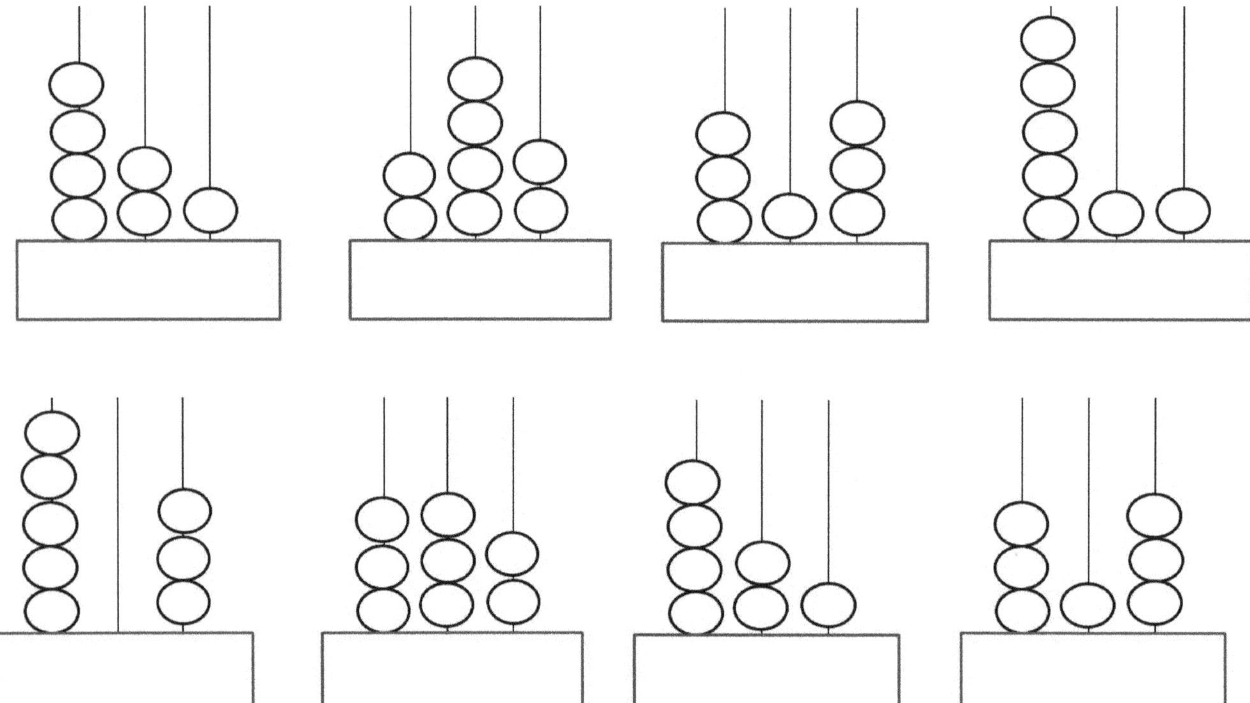

u. Richimon took half of a cake and half of the rest of the cake was taken by Niharika. What part of the cake was taken up by Niharika?

How to write a number!

Four group of tens

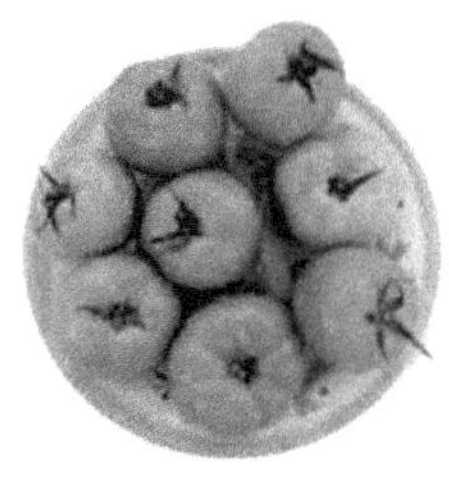

Eight ones

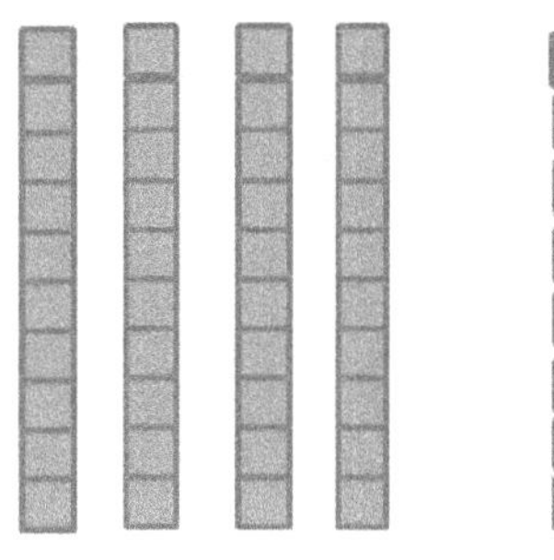

Four stick of tens

Eight ones

There are 48 (Forty eight) fruits.

Tens	Ones
4	8

How many pens are there?

Hundreds	Tens	Ones

Grouping of numbers:

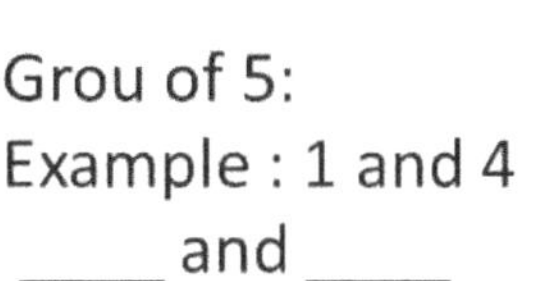

Grou of 6:
Example : 1 and 5
_____ and _____
_____ and _____

Grou of 5:
Example : 1 and 4
_____ and _____
_____ and _____

Count and Write

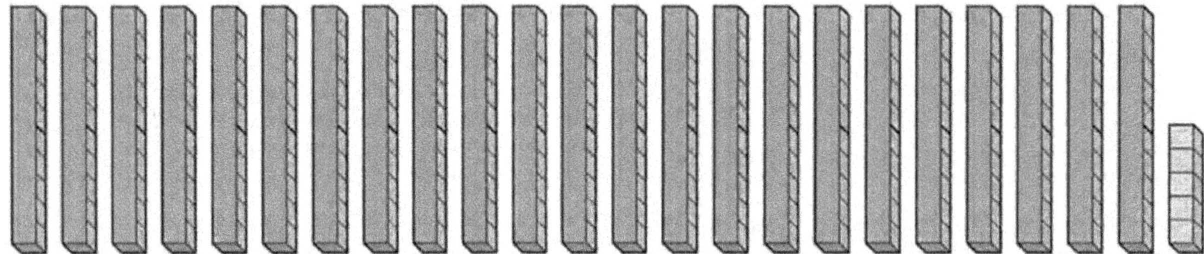

5
ones

23 stick of tens

20 tens + 3 tens = 2 hundreds + 3 tens

Hundreds	Tens	Ones
2	3	5

100s	10s	1s
Hundreds place	Tens place	Ones place

100s	10s	1s
Hund-reds	Tens	Ones

100s	10s	1s
Hundreds place	Tens place	Ones place

100s	10s	1s
Hund-reds	Tens	Ones

Ten ones = 1 ten
Ten tens = 1 hundred

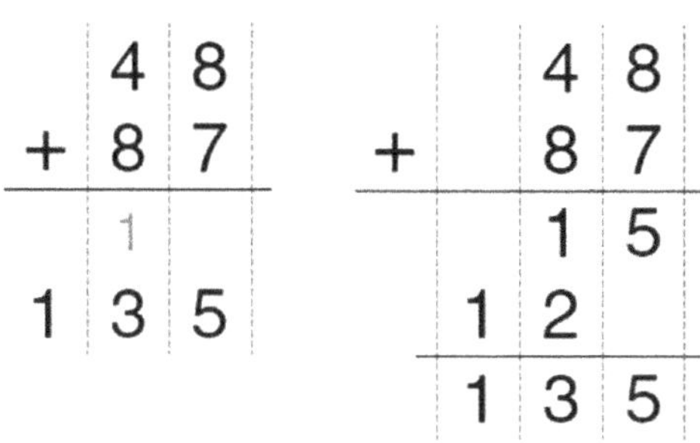

```
    4 8
+   8 7
  ───────
    1
  1 3 5
```

```
      4 8
+     8 7
  ─────────
      1 5
    1 2
  ─────────
    1 3 5
```

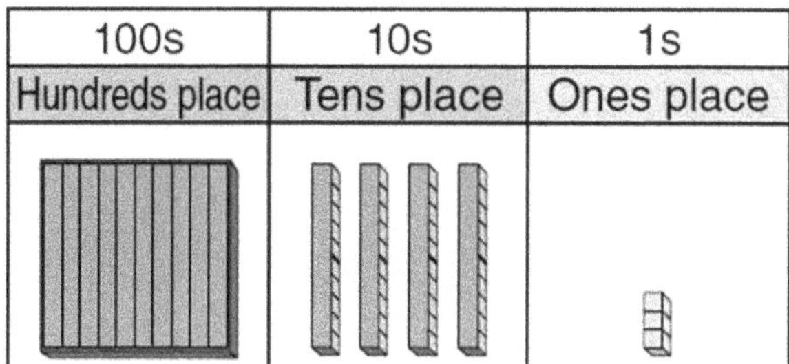

Let us add:

100s	10s	1s
Hundreds place	Tens place	Ones place

+

100s	10s	1s
Hundreds place	Tens place	Ones place

____________ + ____________________ = ____________________.

Calculate the following:

a) 132−41   b) 109−53   c) 146−60

d) 132−47   e) 120−61   f) 106−59

g) 105−58   h) 100−39   i) 102−17

j) 102−7   k) 900−500   l) 1000−200

13 536−5

Model Paper II

1: Nikitha dropped a penny on the floor. Here is the observation:

1. 1st time: tails

2. 2nd time: tails

3. 3rd time: heads

4. 4th time: tails

5. 5th time: heads

6. 6th time: tails

7. 7th time: tails

8. 8th time: heads

How many more times did tails occur than heads? _________

2: Rearrange the following and add: [Hint: 51 + 49 = 100]

51 + 81 + 44 + 39 + 56 + 61 + 19 + 49 = _

3: Which set of numbers is in order from greatest to least?

A 147, 163, 234, 275   B 275, 234, 163, 147

C 275, 163, 234, 147   D 163, 275, 234, 147

4: Which number has a 4 in the tens place and a 4 in the hundreds place?

A 6424   B 6244   C 4462   D 6442

5: 21 hundreds + 21 tens + 21 ones = ___________

6: 100 cm = 1 m then 1010 cm = ___ m _____cm.

7: Predecessor of three digit greatest even number = ______.

8: Represent the fraction equal to a quarter. Als select the correct option.

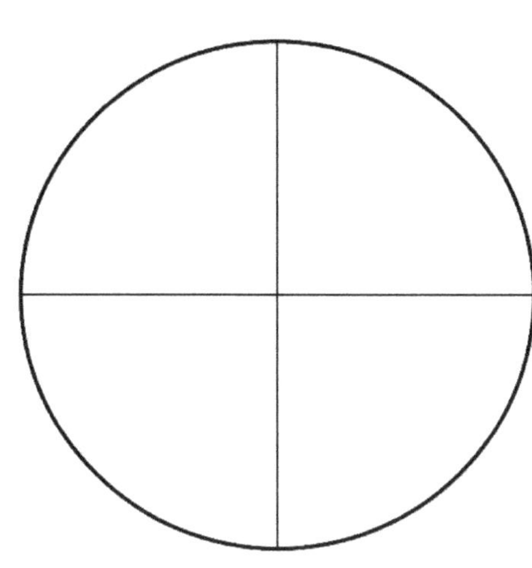

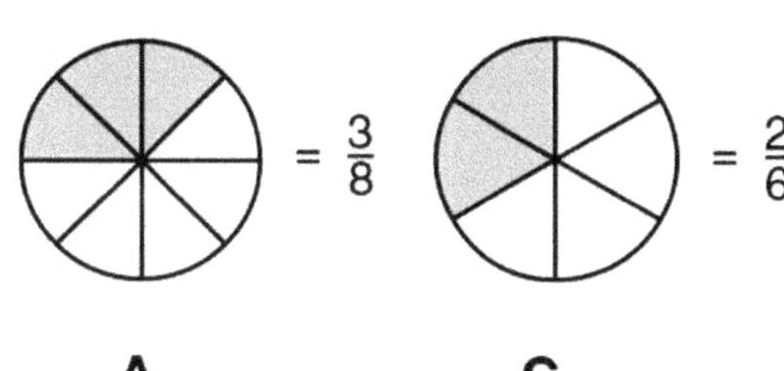

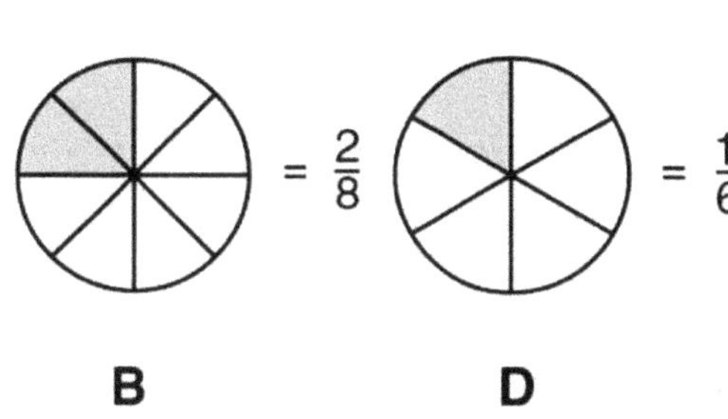

9: Monikornika has $ 15.00 to buy an airplane that costs $14.28. How much change should she get back?

10: Complete the following:

5. 19 + 54 +______	**6.** 39 + 42 +______	**7.** 327 + 581 +______
8. 27 + 78 +______	**9.** 267 + 517 +______	**10.** 465 + 478 +______
11. 186 + 460 +______	**12.** 817 + 118 +______	**13.** 632 + 244 +______

11: one fourth of a cake + three fourth of the same cake

= ______________________ .

Moodel Paper III

1: Addition

1).	T	O		2).	T	O		3).	T	O
	5	5			3	7			9	1
+	4	2		+	2	0		+		2

4).	T	O		5).	T	O
	7	8			2	0
+	1	1		+	5	6

1).	H	T	O		2).	H	T	O		3).	H	T	O
	1	2	4			2	4	1			6	2	0
+	4	7	2		+	7	0	3		+	2	2	2

4).	H	T	O		5).	H	T	O
	5	2	6			4	4	3
+	3	3	1		+		3	5

2: 4,403 − 400 = ________.

3: 4,403 − 4000 = ________.

4: Which number is one more than the successor of smallest four digit odd number?

5: 30,000 + 29 hundreds + 29 tens + 29 ones = ________.

6: Select the correct option:

$$8 \times 4 = 32$$

**Which division sentence is modeled by
the same figure?**
A 8÷4 = 2
B 12 ÷4= 3
C 24 ÷ =3
D 32 ÷8 = 4

7: Second-grade students went to a study tour in 10 buses. Each bus took 55 students. How many students went to the concert?

8: Trace out:

Activities

1: Calculate perimeter of the following:

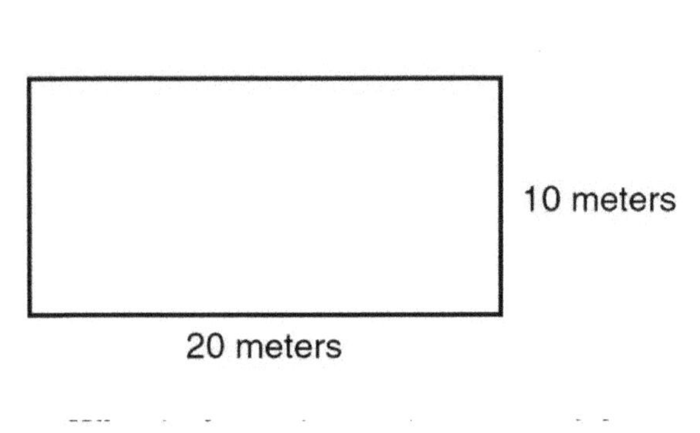

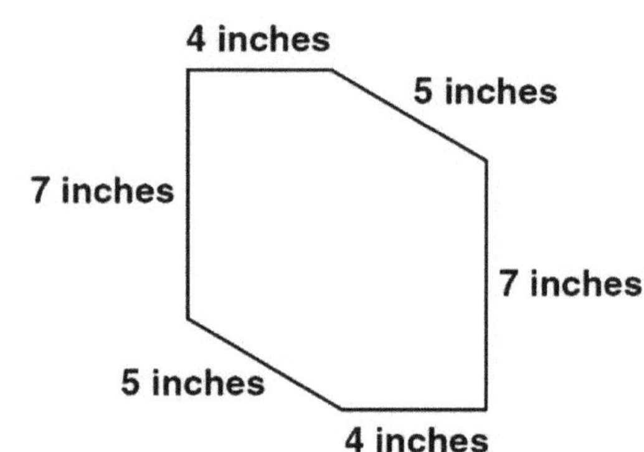

2: 21 X 5 X 20 = ____ X 100.

3: 4 X _____ X 25 = _____ X 60 X 25 = 4 X 60 X ____.

4: 21 thousands + 32 hundreds + 32 tens = _______.

Complete the following number sentences:

5. 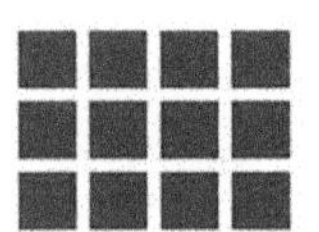

____ X ____ = ____

____ X ____ = ____

6. 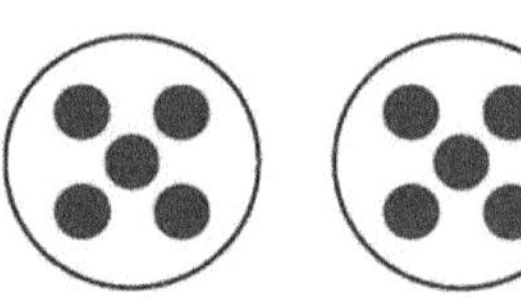

____ X ____ = ____

____ X ____ = ____

7. 

____ X ____ = ____

____ X ____ = ____

8. 3 X 7 = _____ X 3

9. 4 X 5 = 10 X _____

10. 3 X 6 = _____ X 9

11. 6 X _____ = 4 X 9

12. _____ X 8 = 4 X 6

13. 5 X 8 = 8 X _____

14: There are 40 rows each of 6 bird stickers in Mona's sticker album. There are 50 rows each of 5 bird stickers in Paskilla's sticker album. How many bird stickers do they have?

15: Each box holds 6 black markers and 4 red markers. Bhanitelia has 10 boxes of markers. Write a number sentence that shows how many markers Bhanetelia has.

Enrichment –

1. Worksheets

Worksheet 1

1: Write suitable number sentence.

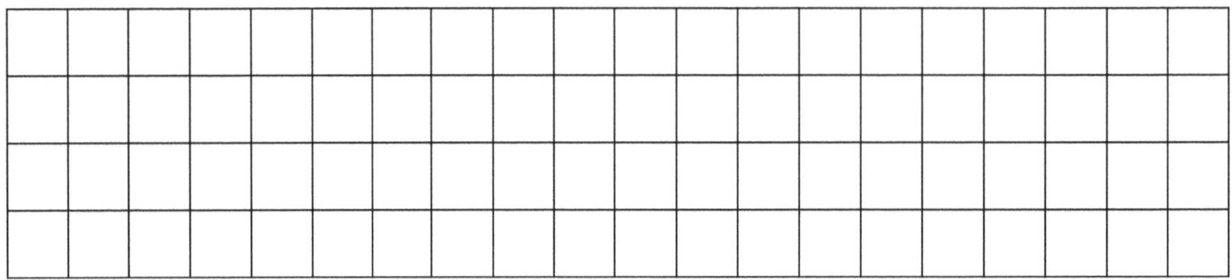

2: Rusty eats 35 cups of food in a week. Mina's dog, Tom, eats few cups of food in a week. Tom eats the same amount each day. In one day, how many more cups of food will Tom eat than Rusty?

3: $2{,}000 + \underline{\qquad} + 50 + 9 = \underline{\qquad\qquad}$.

4: $34 + 66 + 200 + 830 = \underline{\qquad}$.

5: Rijuana walks his dog 21 miles every week. How many miles do they walk in 10 weeks?

Complete the following:

6. $\underline{\quad} = 7 \times 7$ 7. $6 \times 7 = \underline{\quad}$ 8. $\underline{\quad} = 7 \times 10$ 9. $\underline{\quad} = 7 \times 2$

10. $\begin{array}{r} 7 \\ \times 3 \\ \hline \end{array}$	11. $\begin{array}{r} 6 \\ \times 7 \\ \hline \end{array}$	12. $\begin{array}{r} 9 \\ \times 7 \\ \hline \end{array}$	13. $\begin{array}{r} 8 \\ \times 7 \\ \hline \end{array}$	14. $\begin{array}{r} 1 \\ \times 7 \\ \hline \end{array}$	15. $\begin{array}{r} 4 \\ \times 7 \\ \hline \end{array}$
16. $\begin{array}{r} 10 \\ \times 4 \\ \hline \end{array}$	17. $\begin{array}{r} 0 \\ \times 7 \\ \hline \end{array}$	18. $\begin{array}{r} 2 \\ \times 7 \\ \hline \end{array}$	19. $\begin{array}{r} 5 \\ \times 7 \\ \hline \end{array}$	20. $\begin{array}{r} 6 \\ \times 9 \\ \hline \end{array}$	21. $\begin{array}{r} 7 \\ \times 8 \\ \hline \end{array}$

Join Dots:

Find the following:

A: 2 X 8 X 5 = _______ ;

B: 8 X 10 X 2 = _______ ;

Write number sentence:

*	*
*	*
*	*
*	*
*	*
*	*
*	*

There are ___ natural numbers starting from 20 to 80.

Trace the ways out:

Worksheet 2

1: Number Table –

The multiplication table can be used to find products of two numbers.

Example : A = 7 X 2 = 14;   B = 3 X 10 = 30;

$$A + B = 44;$$

Write products for P, Q, R and S and add them.

P + Q   = ________;

P + Q + R   = ________';

P + Q + R + S   = ________;

×	0	1	2	3	4	5	6	7	8	9	10
0											
1											
2								A			
3			P								
4											
5					Q						
6											
7		R							S		
8											
9											
10			B								

2: Calculate by using number table.

A: (4 X 5) + (6 X 5) = ______;

B: 8 X 9 + 9 X 7 = ________;

C: 2 X 5 + 6 X 5 + 7 X 5 = _________;

D: 8 X 8 + 6 X 6 + 4 X 4 = ________;

×	0	1	2	3	4	5	6	7	8	9	10
0	0	0	0	0	0	0	0	0	0	0	0
1	0	1	2	3	4	5	6	7	8	9	10
2	0	2	4	6	8	10	12	14	16	18	20
3	0	3	6	9	12	15	18	21	24	27	30
4	0	4	8	12	16	20	24	28	32	36	40
5	0	5	10	15	20	25	30	35	40	45	50
6	0	6	12	18	24	30	36	42	48	54	60
7	0	7	14	21	28	35	42	49	56	63	70
8	0	8	16	24	32	40	48	56	64	72	80
9	0	9	18	27	36	45	54	63	72	81	90
10	0	10	20	30	40	50	60	70	80	90	100

3: Write in standard form:

A: 2,000 + 500 + 30 + 9 = ________;

B: 34 hundreds + 30 tend + 40 ones = _______;

C: 4,000 + 600 + 80 + 5 = ________;

D: 65 hundreds + 73 tens + 21 = ____________;

E: 50 hundreds + 40 tens + 30 ones + 8 = ______;

3

4: Half of 100 = 10 more than _________.

5: 120 X 21 X 0 X 1,001 X 198 = ______.

6. _____ = 6 × 8   7. 10 × 8 = _____   8. _ = 8 × 3

9. 1 × 8 = _____   10. 4 × 8 = _____   11. 5 × 8 = _____

12. 0 × 8 = _____   13. 8 × 8 = _____   14. 9 X 7 = _____

15. Tom counted 100 coins and placed in 10 different boxes so that each box contain equal number of ocins. There are ______ coins in each box.

16. 21 X 5 X 20 = ______ X 100;

Find the following:

17. $6 \times 5 \times 2$ **18.** $2 \times 3 \times 5$ **19.** $3 \times 1 \times 6$

20. $2 \times 5 \times 6$ **21.** $2 \times 0 \times 8$ **22.** $1 \times 9 \times 4$

23. $2 \times 2 \times 2$ **24.** $4 \times 2 \times 2$ **25.** $2 \times 4 \times 5$

26. $2 \times 6 \times 1$ **27.** $2 \times 9 \times 3$ **28.** $2 \times 7 \times 2$

29. $7 \times (2 \times \underline{\quad}) = 56$ **30.** $30 = 6 \times (5 \times \underline{\quad})$ **31.** $\underline{\quad} \times (2 \times 2) = 32$

32. $42 = 7 \times (2 \times \underline{\quad})$ **33.** $8 \times (5 \times \underline{\quad}) = 40$ **34.** $0 = \underline{\quad} \times (25 \times 1)$

35. $(2 \times 9) \times \underline{\quad} = 18$ **36.** $60 = (2 \times \underline{\quad}) \times 6$ **37.** $4 \times (3 \times \underline{\quad}) = 24$

Path Finders:

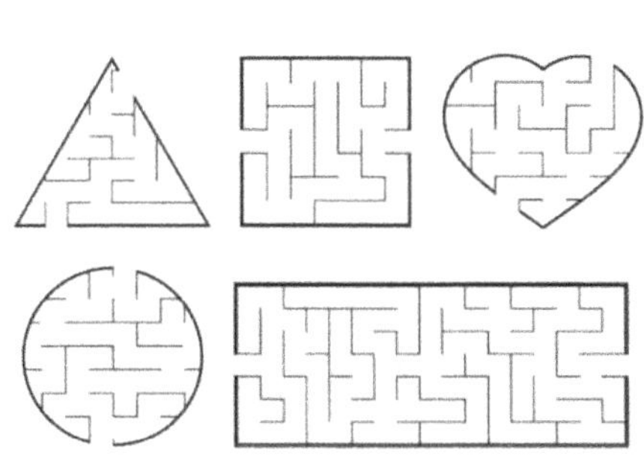
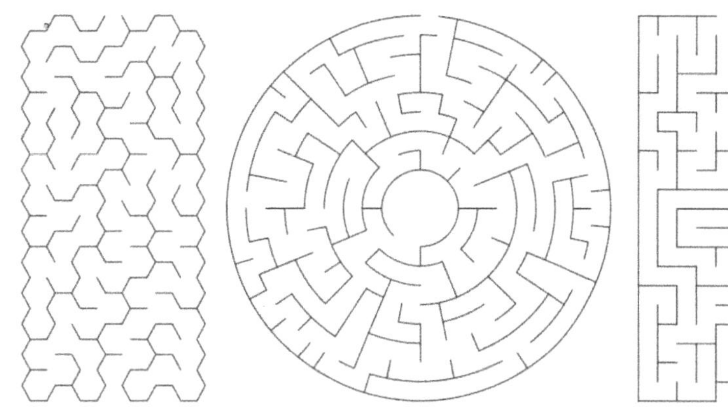

Worksheet 3

1: Use multiplication table to solve the following –

A: (7 X 5) + (6 X 9) = _______;

B: 3 X 9 + 7 X 7 = _________;

C: 2 X 6 + 6 X 6 + 7 X 6 = ___________;

D: 8 X 9 + 6 X 4 + 4 X 3 = _________;

X	0	1	2	3	4	5	6	7	8	9	10
0	0	0	0	0	0	0	0	0	0	0	0
1	0	1	2	3	4	5	6	7	8	9	10
2	0	2	4	6	8	10	12	14	16	18	20
3	0	3	6	9	12	15	18	21	24	27	30
4	0	4	8	12	16	20	24	28	32	36	40
5	0	5	10	15	20	25	30	35	40	45	50
6	0	6	12	18	24	30	36	42	48	54	60
7	0	7	14	21	28	35	42	49	56	63	70
8	0	8	16	24	32	40	48	56	64	72	80
9	0	9	18	27	36	45	54	63	72	81	90
10	0	10	20	30	40	50	60	70	80	90	100

2: Identify –

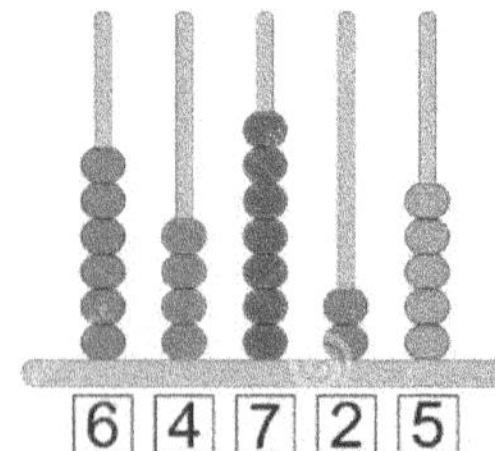
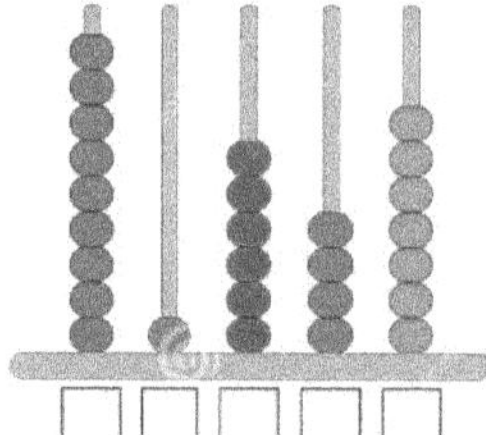
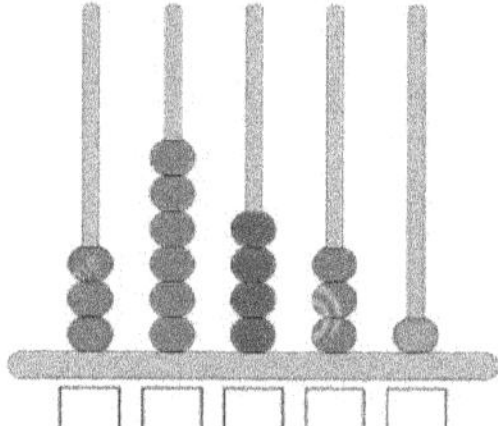
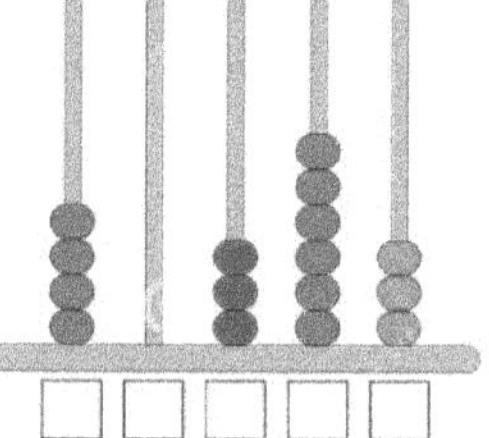

3: Sruti wants to put equal numbers of apples in her frind' baskets. Select the suitable basket from the following.

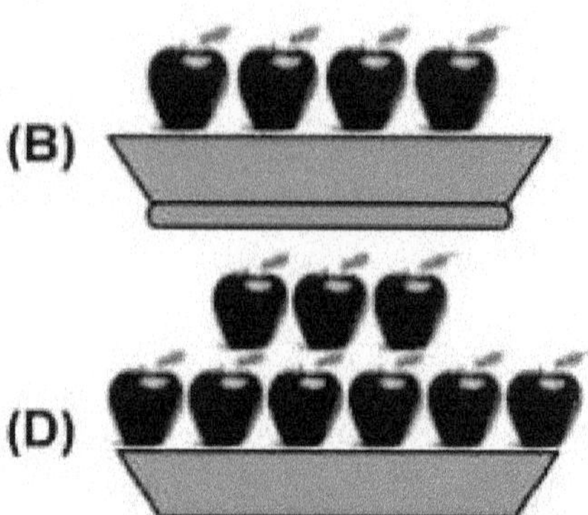

4: 21 hundreds + 21 tens + 21 = _________ .

Find products:

5. $7 \times 20 =$ _____

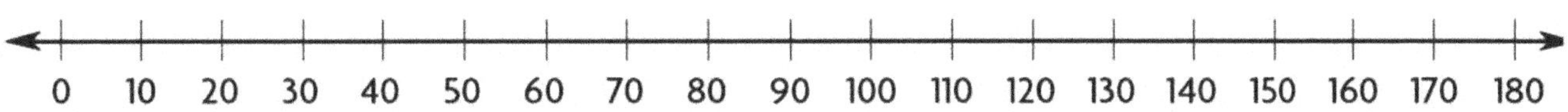

6. $3 \times 50 =$ _____

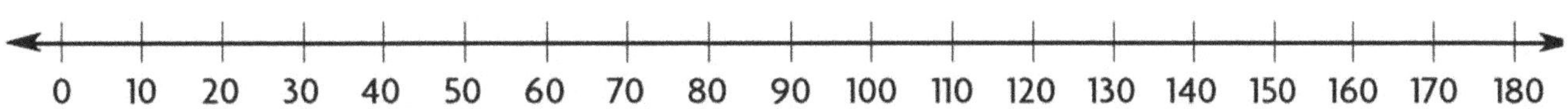

Use place value to find the product.

7. $6 \times 60 = 6 \times$ _____ tens

      $=$ _____ tens $=$ _____

8. $50 \times 7 =$ _____ tens $\times 7$

      $=$ _____ tens $=$ _____

8: Write times displayed by the following clocks.

(A)  (B)  (C)  (D) 

9: Identify fractions –

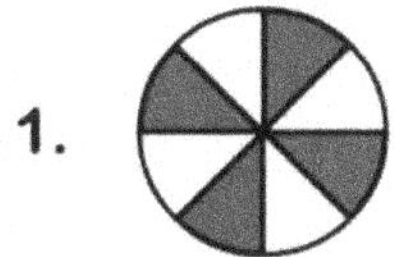

1. $\dfrac{3}{6}$ $\dfrac{3}{5}$ $\left(\dfrac{4}{8}\right)$

2.  $\dfrac{4}{5}$ $\dfrac{1}{3}$ $\dfrac{3}{4}$

3.  $\dfrac{5}{6}$ $\dfrac{3}{7}$ $\dfrac{1}{8}$

4. 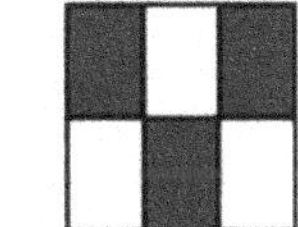 $\dfrac{2}{7}$ $\dfrac{4}{8}$ $\dfrac{3}{6}$

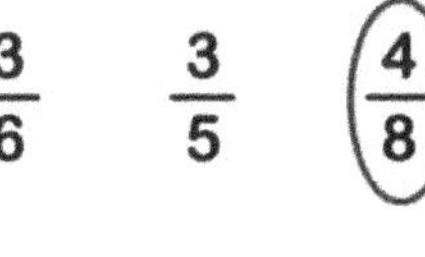
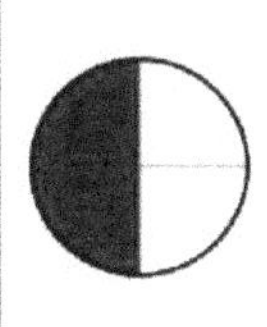 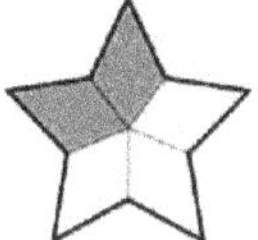  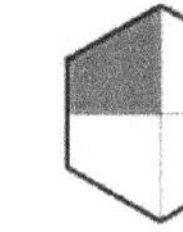
 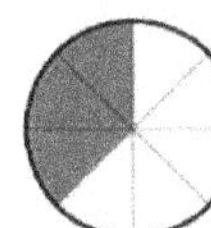 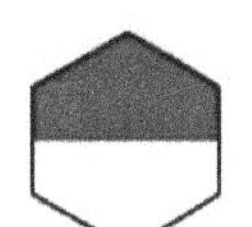 

Enrichment –

Join dots

How many triangles?

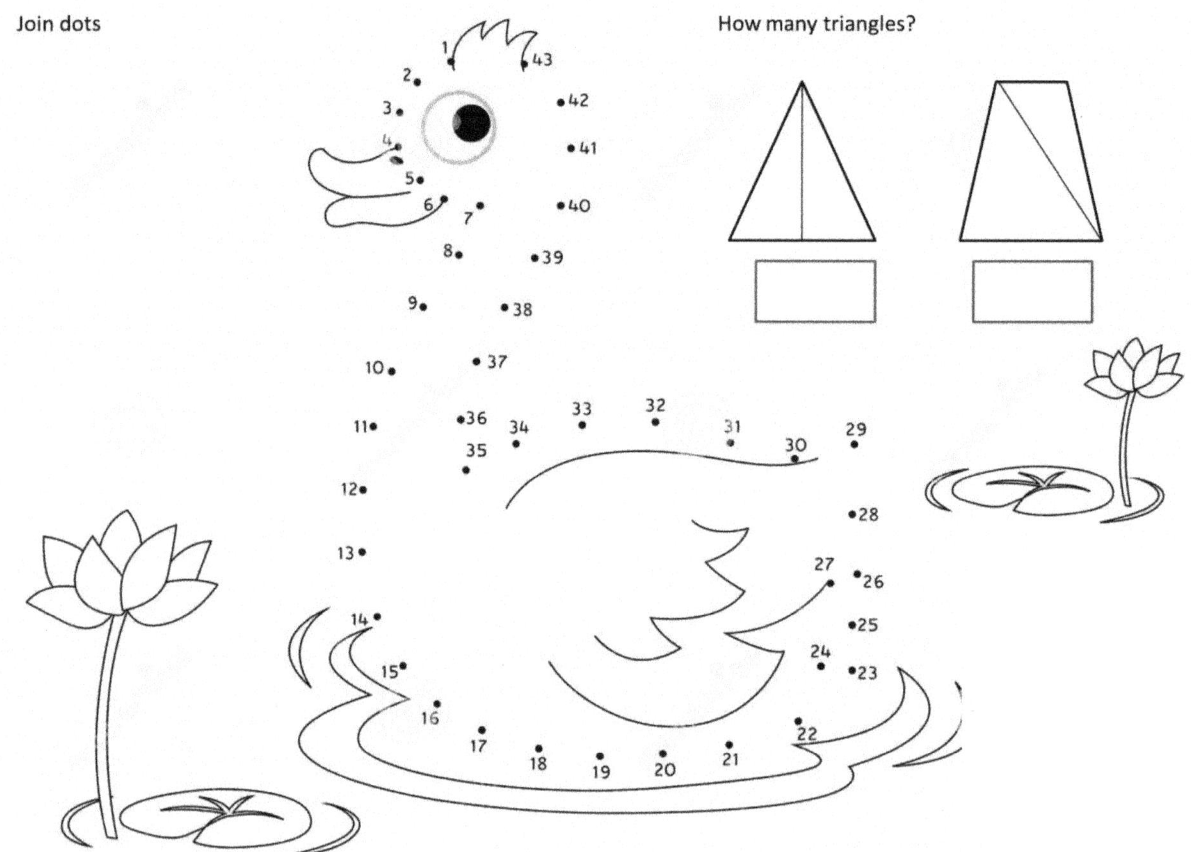

Write a number sentence for the following:

*	*	*	*	*	*	*	*	*	*	*	*	*	*	*	*	*	*	*	*
*	*	*	*	*	*	*	*	*	*	*	*	*	*	*	*	*	*	*	*
*	*	*	*	*	*	*	*	*	*	*	*	*	*	*	*	*	*	*	*
*	*	*	*	*	*	*	*	*	*	*	*	*	*	*	*	*	*	*	*
*	*	*	*	*	*	*	*	*	*	*	*	*	*	*	*	*	*	*	*

______ X ________ = _________;

Join dots:

Worksheet 4

1: What least number must be added to the greatest number of three digits to make it divisible by 10?

2: Write in standard form: 23 hundreds + 32 tens + 65 ones = ___________________.

3. play ball	**4. eat breakfast**	**5. do homework**	**6. sleep**

___________	___________	___________	___________

Find the elapsed time.

7. Start: 10:05 A.M.   End: 10:50 A.M.

10:05

8. Start: 5:30 P.M.
       End: 5:49 P.M.

8: Write values of each of the following fractions.

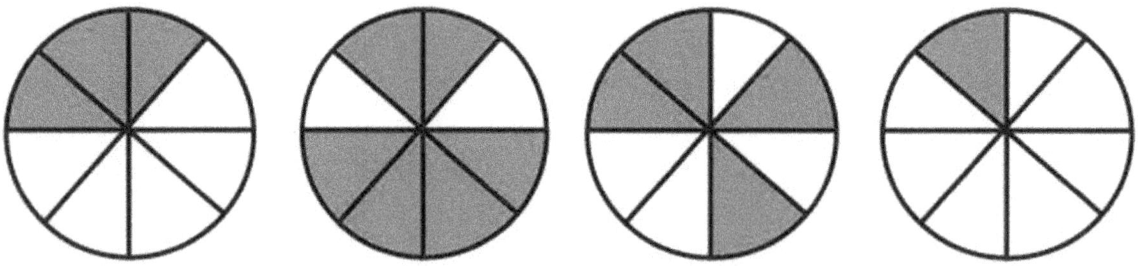

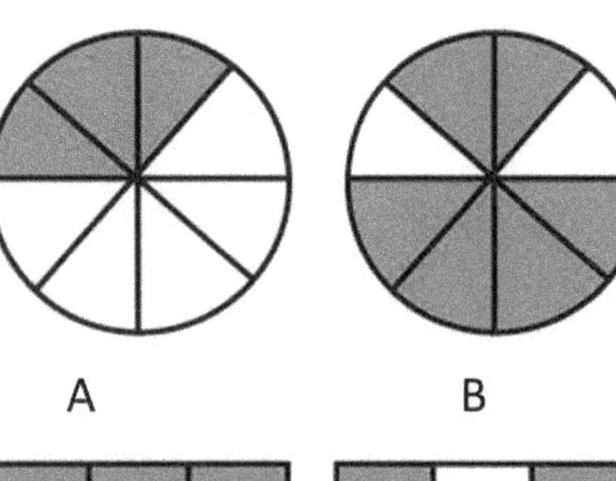

A   B   C   D

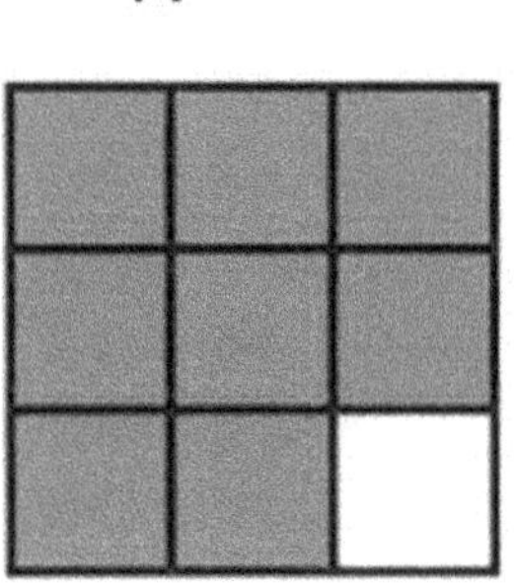
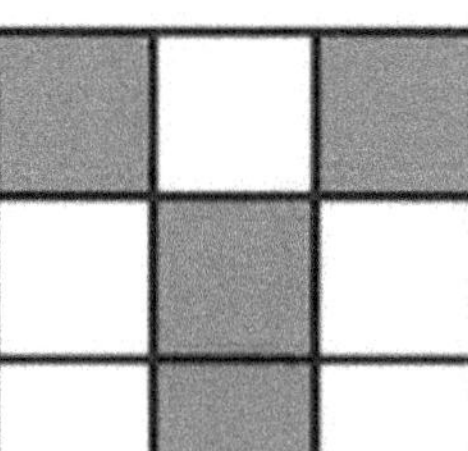
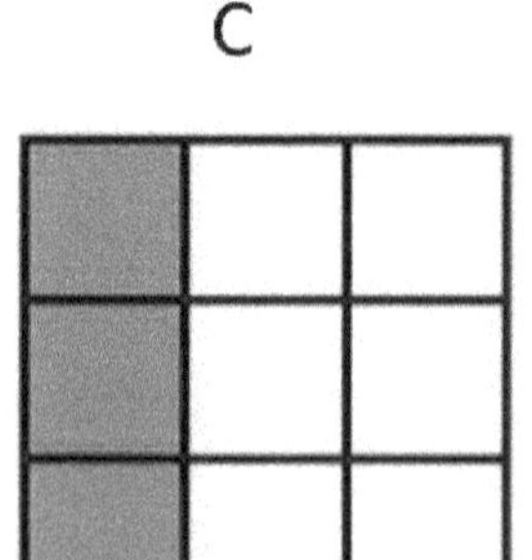
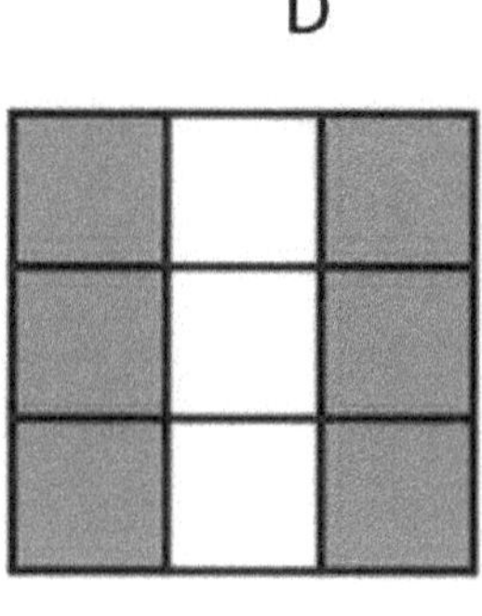

E   F   G   H

9: Write values of each of the following fractions.

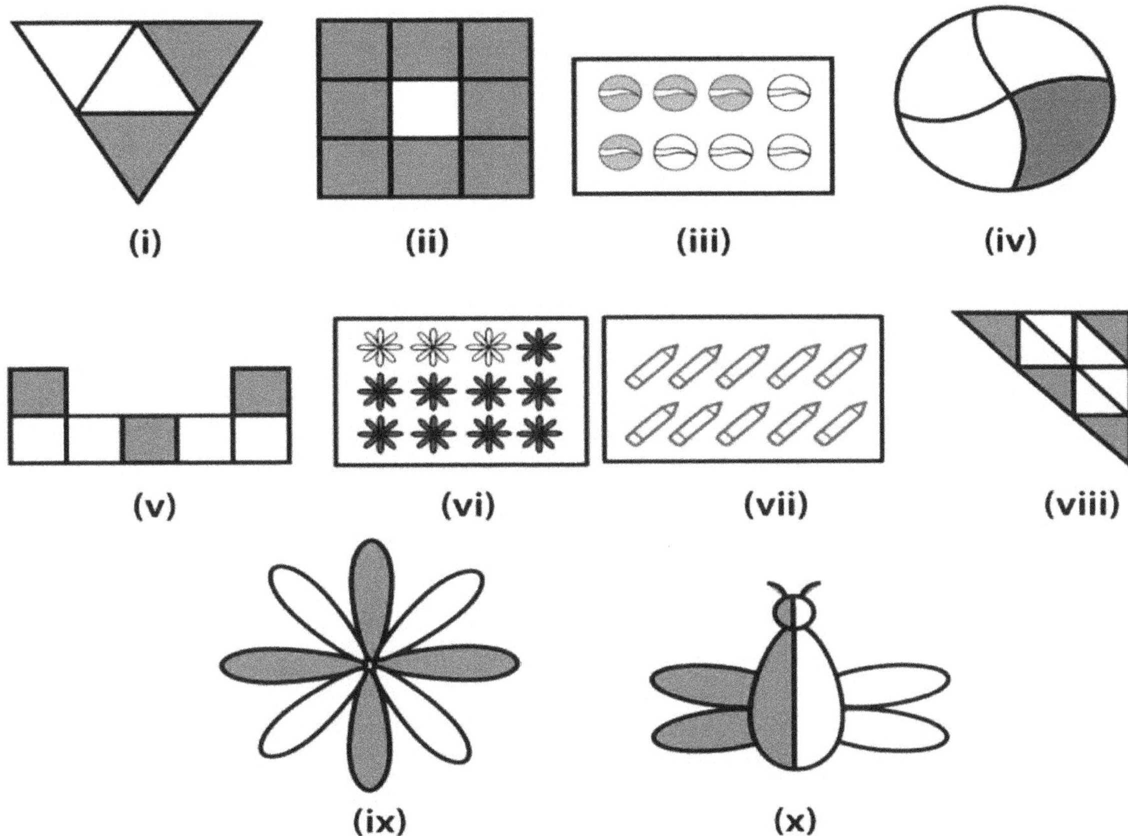

10: Gracy Novalni is going to her friend's house after finishing her soccer game. It takes her 28 minutes to shower and change clothes. Then it takes her 51 minutes to get to her friend's house by car. If her game is over at 4:00 p.m., about what time will she arrive at her friend's house?

11: In December, City of a Hill Station had 3 inches of snow. In January and February that city had 5 inches of snow each month. In March, the city has 2 inches of snow. How many inches of snow fell during December to March?

12: Mhanlal painted a wall in 6 hours. He had 12 such walls more to be painted. He will take _____ days to paint rest of the walls while working 8 hours a day.

13: Sarmishtha has 108 coins to be placed in 9 identical boxes in such a way that equal number of coins should be there in each boxes. Each box will cntain _____ coins.

14: Subtract and check your answer.

1.	500 − 360 _____		**6.**	3,300 − 1,892 _____
2.	800 − 279 _____		**7.**	8,000 − 6,313 _____
3.	$13.00 − $6.37 _____		**8.**	3,000 − 1,811 _____
4.	1,100 − 628 _____		**9.**	$140.00 − $108.92 _____
5.	4,000 − 1,731 _____		**10.**	9,000 − 5,281 _____

Enrichment --

Worksheet 5

Compare the following [use signs such as <. > or =]

1. 1,347 ◯ 1,317

2. 5,781 ◯ 5,872

3. 8,091 ◯ 8,901

4. 11,654 ◯ 1,654

5. 77,215 ◯ 77,215

6. 97,604 ◯ 96,407

7. 111,280 ◯ 112,800

8. 234,582 ◯ 23,458

9. 366,438 ◯ 366,843

10. 672,809 ◯ 672,809

11. 702,593 ◯ 702,359

12. 894,710 ◯ 89,470

13. 1,436,721 ◯ 1,346,721

14. 23,086,543 ◯ 23,806,543

15. 527,308,516 ◯ 523,708,500

16. fifty-two thousand, four hundred sixty-seven ◯ 502,467

17. 800,000 + 60,000 + 400 + 60 + 2 ◯ 97,642

18. Complete the following:

1. 4×4 _____

2. 2×6 _____

3. 5×1 _____

4. 0×7 _____

5. 10×4 _____

6. 2×3 _____

7. 7×2 _____

8. 4×5 _____

9. $3 \div 1$ _____

10. $12 \div 4$ _____

11. $8 \div 2$ _____

12. $15 \div 3$ _____

19: Net Practice attended by Mintonila before taking part in the champions Trophy matches is displayed:

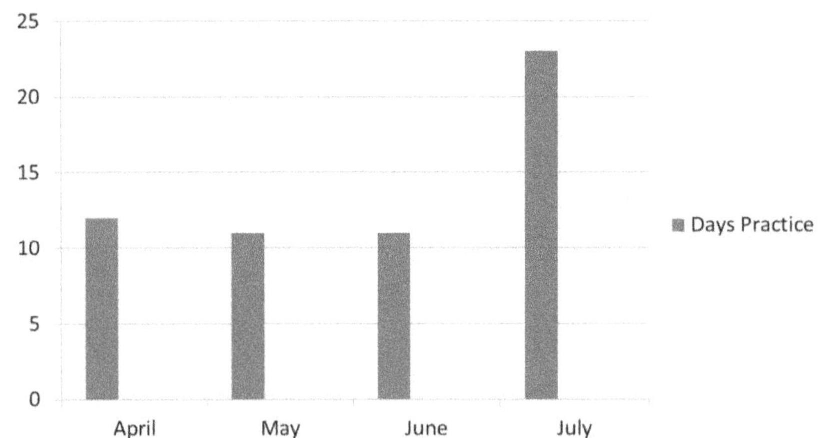

She spent maximum time for doing net ractice during ______________. Tine spent for this purpose during ___________ and ___________ are more or less same.

20: Complete the following –

1. 8 × 2 ______   **2.** 42 ÷ 7 ______

3. 7 × 7 ______   **4.** 72 ÷ 8 ______

5. 6)60 ______   **6.** 5)45 ______

7. 3)21 ______   **8.** 100 ÷ 10 ______

9. 4)40 ______   **10.** 50 ÷ 10 ______

11. 10	**12.** 10	**13.** 5	**14.** 8	**15.** 6
× 7	× 3	× 4	× 5	× 3

21: An express train covers a distance equal to its own length while crossing a passenger standing on platform. The train took 54 seconds to cross a passenger. The train was moving with an average speed of 10 m per second. Length of that train is ________ m.

22. Write in standard form: 32 hundreds + 12 hundreds + 39 tens + 9 = ____________.

Worksheet 6

Rounding up to given place value:

1. 623; ten _______
2. 435; ten _______
3. 581; hundred _______
4. 870; hundred _______
5. 1,302; hundred _______
6. 1,447; hundred _______
7. 2,398; thousand _______
8. 4,628; thousand _______
9. 23,876; thousand _______
10. 31,098; thousand _______
11. 44,872; ten thousand _______
12. 65,281; ten thousand _______
13. 124,830; ten thousand _______
14. 237,524; hundred thousand _______
15. 497,320; hundred thousand _______
16. 1,567,438; hundred thousand _______
17. 2,802,746; hundred thousand _______
18. 3,458,321; thousand _______
19. 4,872,018; ten thousand _______
20. 6,873,652; thousand _______

Q 21: Somalia got three collections of gift cards in such a way that number of cards in the first group was equal to the three digit smallest odd number, second group was containing 300 more cards than group 1 and third group was there with 150 moore cards than that with the first group. She arranged all the cards in a single group. Total cards in her collection will be _______.

<u>Aid Box:The Number System</u>

Write each number in standard form.

1. 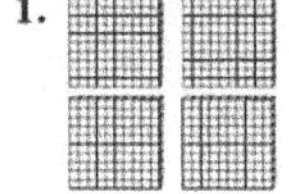   2. 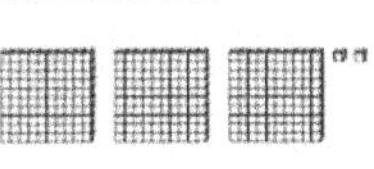   3.

_______   _______   _______

4. 300 + 40 + 9 _______

5. 100 + 60 + 3 _______

6. 700 + 90 + 9 _______

7. seven hundred eighty _______

8. six hundred thirty-two _______

10. Roselina added 21 hundreds , 43 hundreds to the smallest number of four digits. Find the digit which will be there at thousands place of the result.

9. Expand the following.

A: 3,432 = _______ + _______ + _____ + _____

A: 8.014 = _______ + _______ + _____ + _____

A: 3,005 = _______ + _______ + _____ + _____

A: 8,765 = _______ + _______ + _____ + _____

A: 4,564 = _______ + _______ + _____ + _____

A: 4,090 = _______ + _______ + _____ + _____

A: 1,009 = _______ + _______ + _____ + _____

A: 2,435 = _______ + _______ + _____ + _____

Worksheet 7

1: Alonso earns $6 each day walking his aunt's dog. He is saving to buy a mountain bike helmet for $24. How many days will Alonso need to work to buy his mountain bike helmet?

2: Sardana needs to leave in 1 h 25 minutes to go to a talk show. Before he leaves, he has to finish his homework, which takes 22 minutes; clean his room, which takes 15 minutes; walk the dog, which takes 25 minutes; and take out the trash, which takes 3 minutes. Does Sardana have enough time to do all of these before he leaves for the talk show?

3. Expand: 32,043 = _________ + _______ + _________ + ______ + _____.

4. Every night Piskilla reads for 20 minutes before going to sleep. How many minutes does Anna read in 5 weeks?

5. Gresi's sunflower is 12 inches taller than her sister Nimmi's plant. If Nimmi's plant is 44 inches tall, how tall is Gresi's sunflower?

6. Graff's basketball games comprise 4 quarters that are each 12 minutes long. Is it possible for Graff to play 45 minutes in a game? She needs _____ minutes extra.

7: Solve the following:

Write in standard form.

1. 30,000 + 5,000 + 300 + 20 + 1   2. 40,000 + 9,000 + 400 + 70 + 2

_________________________   _________________________

3. 20,000 + 3,000 + 500 + 6   4. 80,000 + 800 + 8

_________________________   _________________________

5. 70,000 + 200 + 80 + 9   6. 10,000 + 4,000 + 600 + 90 + 4

_________________________   _________________________

7. sixty-one thousand, eight hundred thirty-one   8. forty-three thousand, five hundred forty-five

_________________________   _________________________

Write the value of the underlined digit.

9. 91,643   10. 36,955   11. 72,561

_________________ _________________ _________________

Worksheet 8

Complete the following:

1. 11×6 _____

2. $12 \div 3$ _____

3. $5\overline{)55}$ _____

4. 3×12 _____

5. $44 \div 4$ _____

6. $12\overline{)60}$ _____

7. 5×11 _____

8. $99 \div 9$ _____

9. $11\overline{)88}$ _____

10. 12×8 _____

11. $96 \div 12$ _____

12. $5\overline{)60}$ _____

13. $\begin{array}{r} 11 \\ \times\ 5 \\ \hline \end{array}$

14. $\begin{array}{r} 11 \\ \times\ 3 \\ \hline \end{array}$

15: Choose a number range of 10 , 25, 50, 100 or 500 to estimate each of the following .

1. the number of doors in your home   = 10 (example)

2. the number of fire crackers in a large box

3. the number of hours in your school day

4. the number of pages in a book of sports stories

5. the number of players on a baseball team

6. the number of desks in your classroom

7. the number of seats in a professional sports stadium

8. the number of shopping carts at a large supermarket

9. the number of slices in a loaf of bread

10. the number of days in three months

11. the number of books in your school bag

12. the number of crayons in your colour box

13. the number of pencils and pens in your pencil box

Mixed Review

16: Write the type of symmetry displayed by following figures.

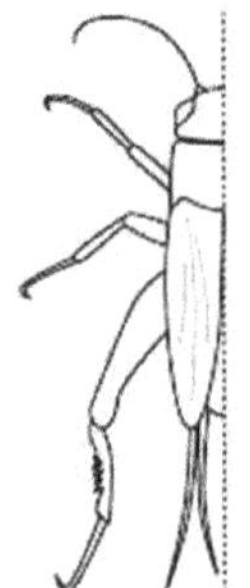 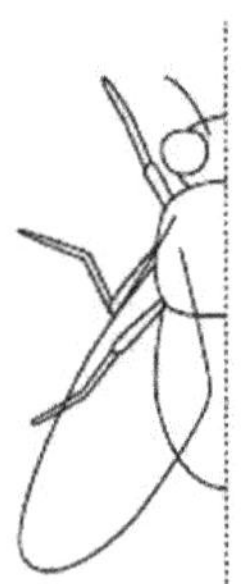 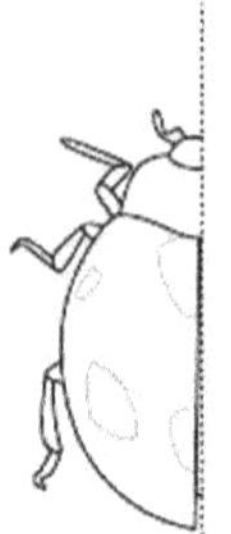 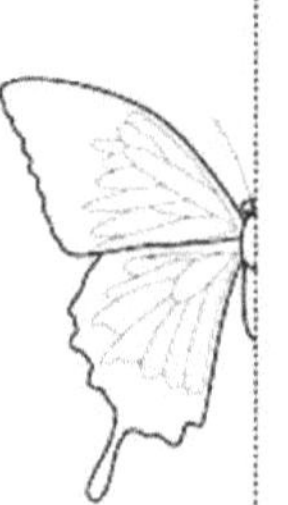

17: Sobjhonsky earned 367 points on the first level of a board game. He earned 133 more points on the second level than the first. How many total points did Sobjhonsky earn after two levels?

18: 25 X 4 = 100; 20 X 5 = 100;   4 X 121 X 25 = ______;   5 X 121 X 20 = ___;

19: A teacher wants to buy 4 new basketballs for each class in 2 schools. Each school has 4 elementary classes and 5 middleschool classes. How many basketballs does the teacher need to buy?

20: Complete the following.

Let's calculate in vertical form.

① 324 + 253   ② 146 + 537   ③ 473 + 261

④ 246 + 485   ⑤ 354 + 249   ⑥ 464 + 368

⑦ 658 − 325   ⑧ 374 − 138   ⑨ 546 − 369

⑩ 432 − 136   ⑪ 604 − 247   ⑫ 700 − 463

Let's calculate in vertical form.

① 734 + 862   ② 947 + 587   ③ 457 + 546

④ 4137 + 1425   ⑤ 2056 + 3794   ⑥ 2361 + 7639

⑦ 1529 − 716   ⑧ 1153 − 645   ⑨ 1000 − 437

⑩ 3947 − 1925   ⑪ 3142 − 1734   ⑫ 10000 − 4005

Let's calculate.

① 5387 + 57 + 43   ② 26 + 3285 + 74

Write a suitable number sentence.

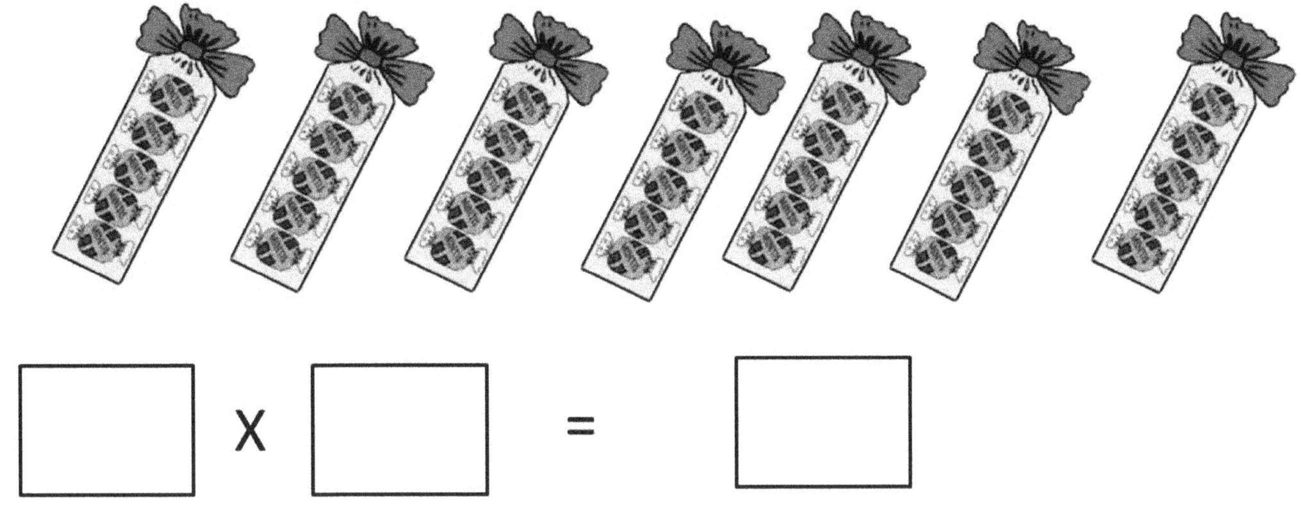

☐ X ☐ = ☐

Trace out another half of the following figures:

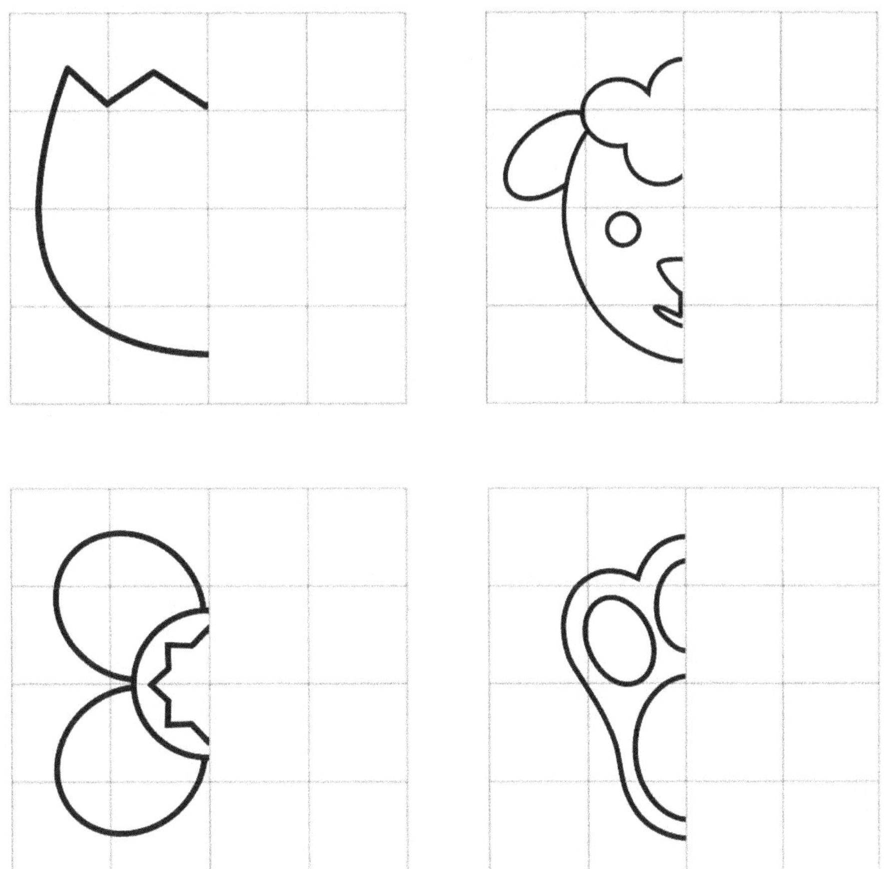

Worksheet 9

1. 73 × 3 = _______   **2.** 88 × 4 = _______   17. Write a number sentence.

3. 44 × 5 = _______   **4.** 74 × 5 = _______

5. 31 × 7 = _______   **6.** 85 × 4 = _______

7. 68 × 8 = _______   **8.** 77 × 6 = _______

9. 32 × 9 = _______   **10.** 97 × 2 = _______

11. 65 × 5 = _______   **12.** 66 × 8 = _______

13. 33 × 6 = _______   **14.** 94 × 3 = _______

15. 96 × 3 = _______   **16.** 59 × 7 = _______   ___ X _____ = _______

18: Write True or False.

a) There are eight prime numbers in between 1 and 20.

b) All prime numbers has only one factor.

c) All composite numbers has more than two factors.

d) 69 is a multiple of 1, 3 and 23.

e) There is only one prime number in between 90 and 100.

f) Sum total of 21 hundredths and 543 thousandths is greater than 1.

g) All natural numbers are not composite numbers.

h) Any number divisible by 5 should have digit 0 or 5 at its one's place.

i) Any number divisible by 8 is also divisible separately by all the other factors of 8, 4 and 2.

19. Difference of digits of a two digit number is 7. if digits are reversed then sum total of both the number becomes the predecessor of the three digit smallest number. Find the second multiple of this number.

A: 45   B: 18   C: 36   D: 81

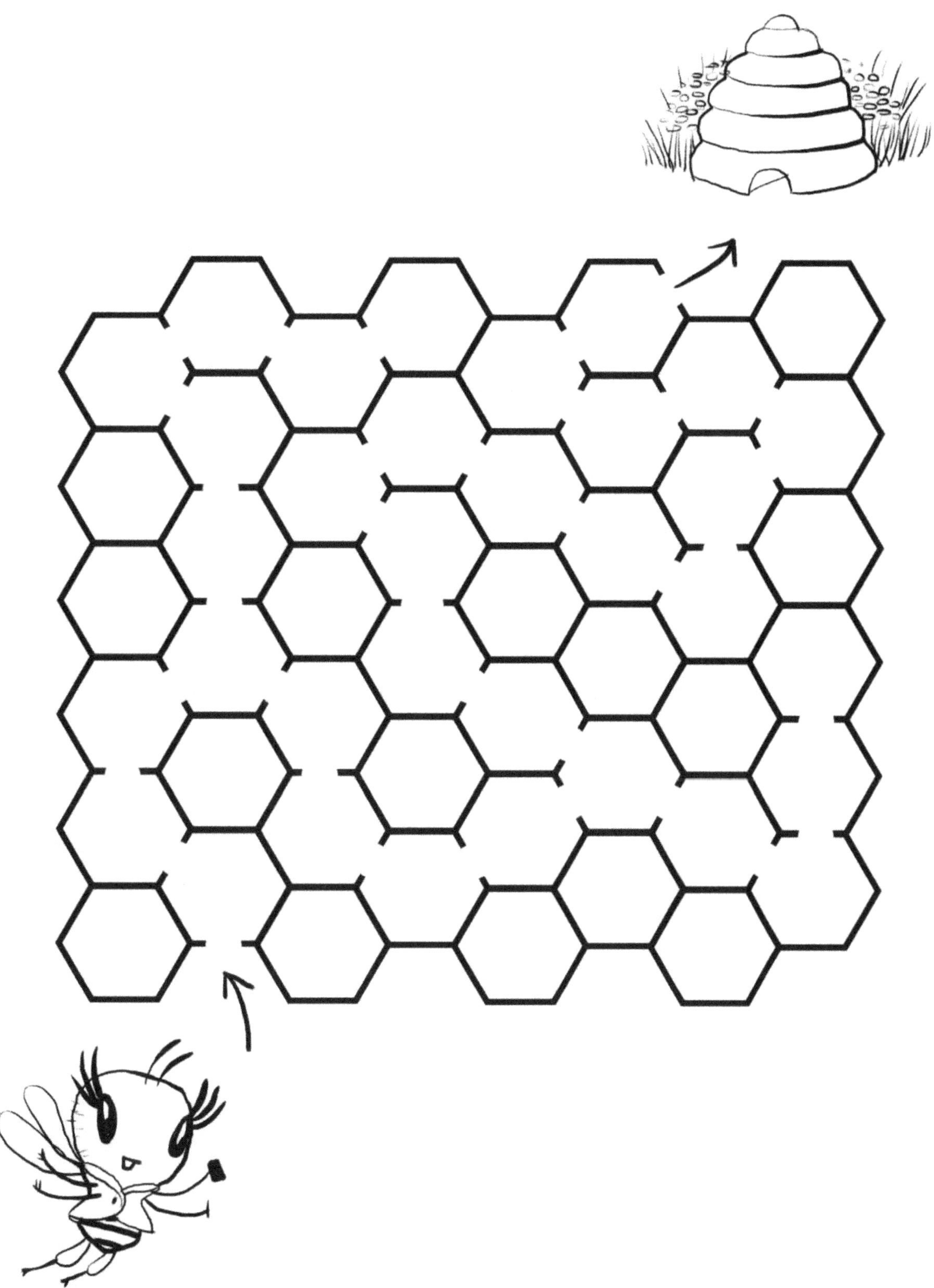

Worksheet 10

1. 5 + 5 + 5 + …… 100 times = 5 X ______ = __________

2. 5 X 20 = 100;   101 X 5 X 20 = __________.

3. 50 times 12 = ______ X ______ = ____ X 100.

4. 55 × 5 = ______	**10.** 4 × 52 = ______	**16.** 9 × 22 = ______
5. 75 × 6 = ______	**11.** 63 × 7 = ______	**17.** 72 × 8 = ______
6. 8 × 47 = ______	**12.** 29 × 9 = ______	**18.** 33 × 5 = ______
7. 6 × 39 = ______	**13.** 32 × 5 = ______	**19.** 2 × 90 = ______
8. 2 × 98 = ______	**14.** 4 × 60 = ______	
9. 84 × 6 = ______	**15.** 66 × 8 = ______	

Aid Box

Write in standard form:

   a. Three hundreds + 32 tens + 21   = __________ ;

   b. 454 + 43 tens + 21 tenths   = __________ ;

   c. 21 thousands + 21 thousandths   = __________ ;

   d. 21 hundreds + 21 tenths + 21 hundredths   = __________ ;

   e. 1,202 + 2,002 + 12,009   = __________ ;

   f. 1.004 + 10.04 + 100.4   = __________ ;

   g. Ten thousands + 10 hundredths   = __________ ;

   h. 21 thousand + 12 million   = __________ ;

CITY PARK

2. Daily Practice

Worksheet 1

1: About 450 thousands people lived in Mangalore in 2000. In 2005, about 467 thousands people lived in Mangalore. Did the number of people living in the city get larger or smaller? Find the difference.

2: Rounak scored 20 marks more in Mathematics and 12 markes less in SST that the marks obtained in Science. Score of Science was 78. Find his scores in SST and Mathematics.

3: Observe the order in which students are standing before entering a sports complex.

Mohit and Gautam interchange their position

Find the position of Gautam after the interchange. What will be the position of Mohit from right hand side after the interchange?

4: Perform the following multiplication.

$1 \times 5 = 5$
1 multiplied by 5 equals 5

$2 \times 5 = \boxed{}$
2 multiplied by 5 equals 10

$\boxed{} \times \boxed{} = \boxed{}$

$\boxed{} \times \boxed{} = \boxed{}$

$\boxed{} \times \boxed{} = \boxed{}$

5: Identify following numbers and arrange the numbers in ascending order.

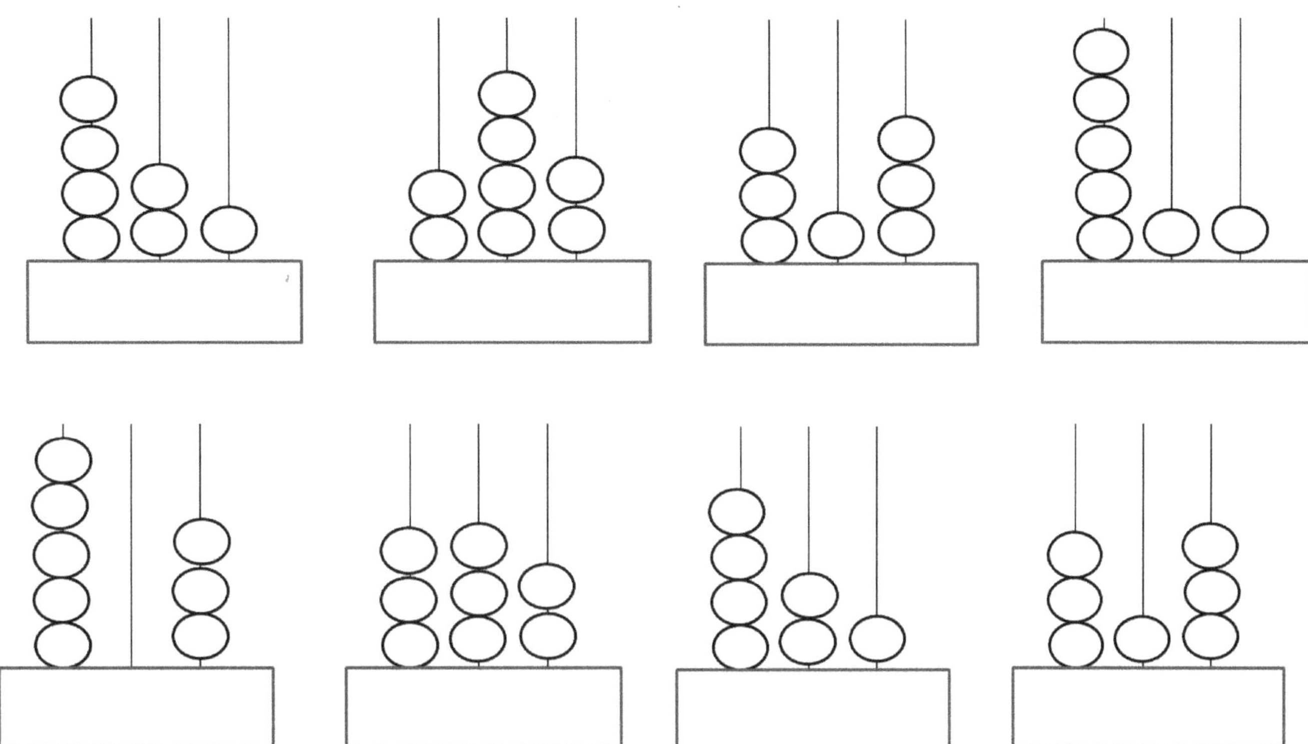

Enrichment: How many more blocks required in each case for making cuboidal patterns comlpete?

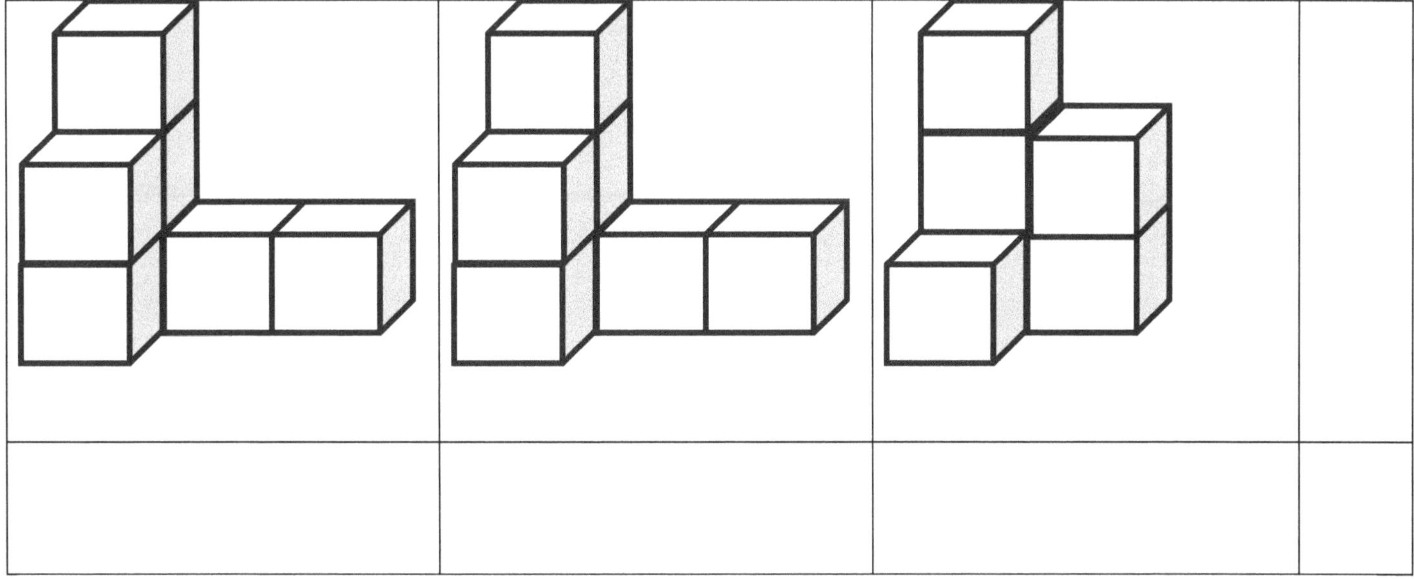

Aid Box: Complete the following Basic Operations .

1. $5 \times 3 =$ _____   2. $3 \times 5 =$ _____

+—+→
0 2 4 6 8 10 12 14 16 18 20 22 24 26 28 30 32 34 36 38 40 42 44 46 48 50

3. $5 \times 5 =$ _____   4. $4 \times 3 =$ _____   5. $9 \times 3 =$ _____   6. $2 \times 3 =$ _____

7. $4 \times 5 =$ _____   8. $3 \times 8 =$ _____   9. $7 \times 2 =$ _____   10. $3 \times 3 =$ _____

11. $9 \times 5 =$ _____   12. $6 \times 3 =$ _____   13. $2 \times 2 =$ _____   14. $5 \times 3 =$ _____

15. $8 \times 2 =$ _____   16. $5 \times 9 =$ _____   17. $2 \times 9 =$ _____   18. $6 \times 5 =$ _____

19. $5 \times 4 =$ _____   20. $3 \times 9 =$ _____   21. $5 \times 2 =$ _____   22. $7 \times 3 =$ _____

23. $8 \times 5 =$ _____   24. $7 \times 5 =$ _____   25. $2 \times 5 =$ _____

26. $5 \times 8 =$ _____   27. $3 \times 4 =$ _____   28. $2 \times 7 =$ _____

29. $3 \times 6 =$ _____   30. $9 \times 2 =$ _____   31. $8 \times 4 =$ _____

Circle the letter for the correct answer.

32. $24 + 56 + 12 =$ ▣   33. $17 + 11 + 45 =$ ▣   34. $12 + 9 + 19 =$ ▣

35. Somalina arranged 1600 different cards in a grid having 8 columns. How many rows will be formed in that grid? Her friend Tintolina took 32 cards. Now find the total number of rows in the newly reared grid having 8 columns.

36. $(12 + 12 + \ldots\ldots 1{,}000 \text{ times}) + (28 + 28 + \ldots\ldots 1{,}000 \text{ times}) =$ _________________.

37. Half of a number exceeds four digit smallest number by 11. Find the number.

38. 43 hundreds + 32 tens + 65 tens + 32 ones = _______________.

***.

Worksheet 2

1: Write in standard form: 43 hundreds + 57 hundreds + 87 tens = ______________.

2: (43 X 100) + (57 X 100) + (89 X 100) + (11 X 100) = ______________.

3: Complete the following:

      1, 3, 5, ____, _____, ______, ______, ______, ______, ______, 21, ______, _____.

4: Find the greatest two digit number which is divisible by 2.

5: One fifth of 5,050 = _________.

6: Observe the following figures displaying three isosceles triangles along with their lines of symmetry –

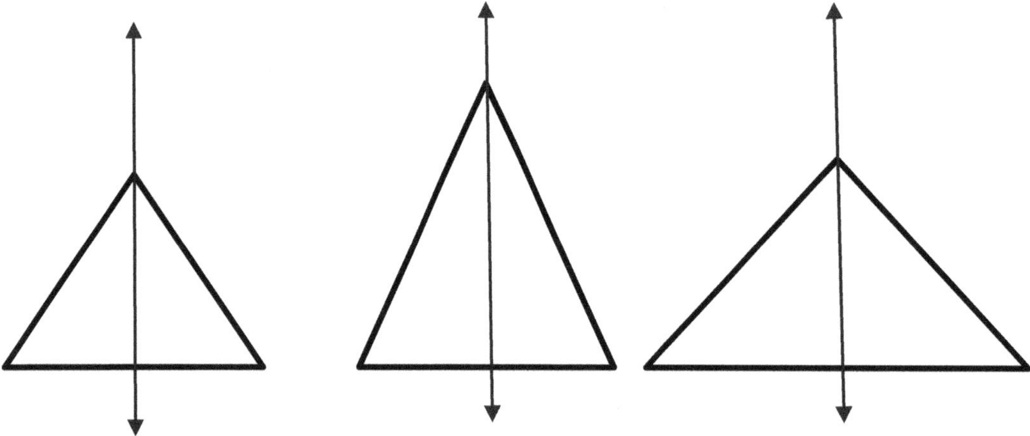

All these 3 triangles have several common things.

Identify them

A: They have only one line of symmetry.

B: Two sides out of three in each triangle are equal to each other.

C: Line of symmetry in each triangle bisects the vertex angle,

D: They are identical shapes by all means (in terms of sides and angles).

Which of the statements are not true?

7: Students in play ground enjoyed a lot while doing Yoga.

A: How many girls took part in the session?

B: How many columns and how many rows are there?

C: Prepare a number sentence to calculate the number of students.

8: Observe the diagram in which four triangles are displayed. All these triangles have two sides equal to each other –

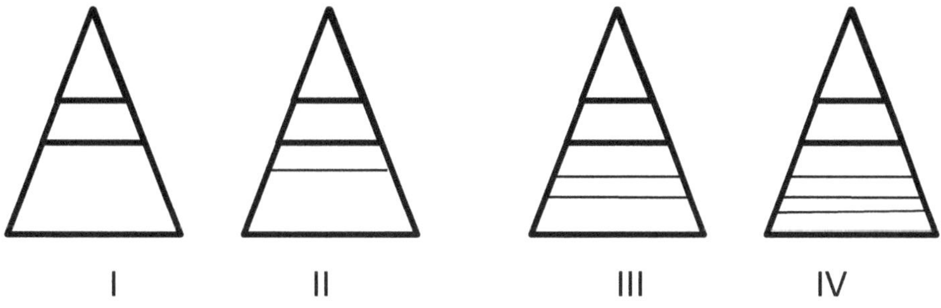

Identify the type of pattern.

    a. Number of triangles increasing continuously.

    b. Each time there is an increase of one triangle.

    c. In seventh pattern the number of triangles will be 9.

    d. Area of the greatest triangle remains unchanged.

    e. All the triangles are of isosceles type.

Which of the statements are not true?

9: . Complete the number pattern:

       1, 4, 9, 16, ………, …………., ……………., ……………

10: Cost of 2 pens and 3 pencils is $ 7. In another combination cost of 3 pens and 2 pencils is $ 13. Calculate the cost of a new pack containing 15 pens and 15 pencils of such type?

11. In 29th December 2019 it   was Sunday. The following Monday was ___________January 2020.

12. The product of 11th multiple of 100 and the 19th multiple of 108 has _________ at its one's place and ________________ at its ten's place.

13. 35 × 10 ___________	**14.** $723 × 20 _________
15. $58 × 40 _____________	**16.** 448 × 40 _________
17. $89 × 30 _____________	**18.** 58 × 60 _________
19. 54 × 80 _____________	**20.** 98 × 80 _________
21. 43 × 40 _____________	**22.** $51 × 50 _________
23. 45 × 80 _____________	**24.** $663 × 30 _________
25. 99 × 90 _____________	**26.** 39 × 70 _________
27. 75 × 50 _____________	**28.** 87 × 20 _________

29. Write multiplication sentence

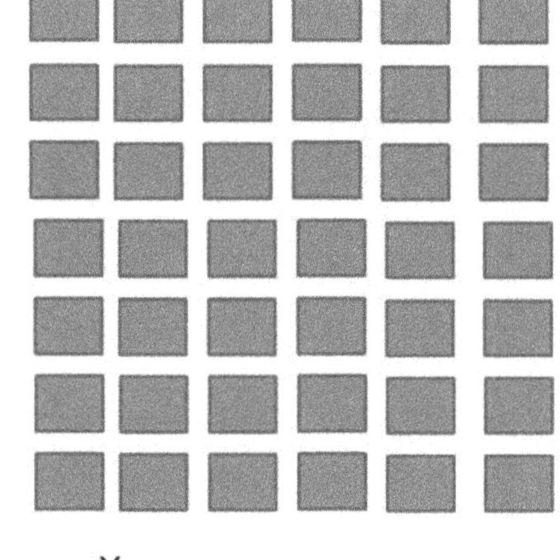

________ X ________ = ____________

30. If 306 X 10 = 3,000 + 60, then

306 X 1000 = _____________ + __________

31: There are 72 times for students to work in the computer lab during one week. If 30 students can work in the computer lab at one time, about how many students can work in the computer lab during four weeks?

32: Observe the figure and select correct options.

a. It is not a polygon.

b. It has 6 sides.

c. It is not an octagon.

d. It is a regular polygon.

e. It has six lines of symmetry.

f. Each lines of symmetry divides the figure into two equal halves.

Which of the above statements are not true?

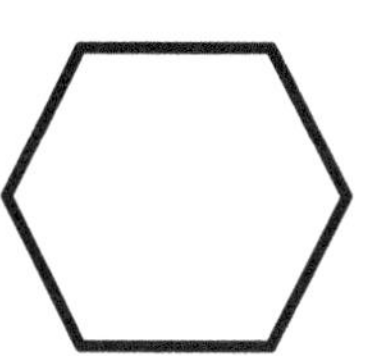

33: 196,547 X 20,405 = A; Digits at ten's and one's place of A are respectively __ and __.

Aid Box:

1: (5 + 5 + ... 1000 times) = 5 X _______ = ___________ .

2. 4 × 6 = _____   3. 3 × 8 = _____   4. 6 × 2 = _____

5. 5 × 4 = _____   6. 8 × 6 = _____   7. 6 × 5 = _____

8. 7 × 6 = _____   9. 3 × 9 = _____   10. 6 × 6 = _____

11. 6 × 0 = _____   12. 1 × 6 = _____   13. 4 × 9 = _____

14. 9   15. 7   16. 6   17. 3
   ×6   ×4   ×3   ×4

Complete the multiplication table.

18.	×	1	2	3	4	5	6	7	8	9
	6	___	___	___	___	___	___	___	___	___

Worksheet 3

1. 460 × 6 = ________

2. 308 × 8 = ________

3. 6,404 × 3 = ________

4. 5,060 × 5 = ________

5. 7,032 × 4 = ________

6. 3,056 × 6 = ________

7. 7,501 × 4 = ________

8. 7,810 × 8 = ________

9. $2,058 × 3 = ________

10. $8,040 × 2 = ________

12. Write number sentence.

_____ X _____ = _____

11. Multiply by 5,809.

Input	5	6	7	8	9
Output					

12: Write division sentences.

Pandemonelia started sorting cards in the fashion displayed below for regrouping . She wants to make new arrangements by using all these cards. Write present and newly prepared division sentence for collection of all these cards.

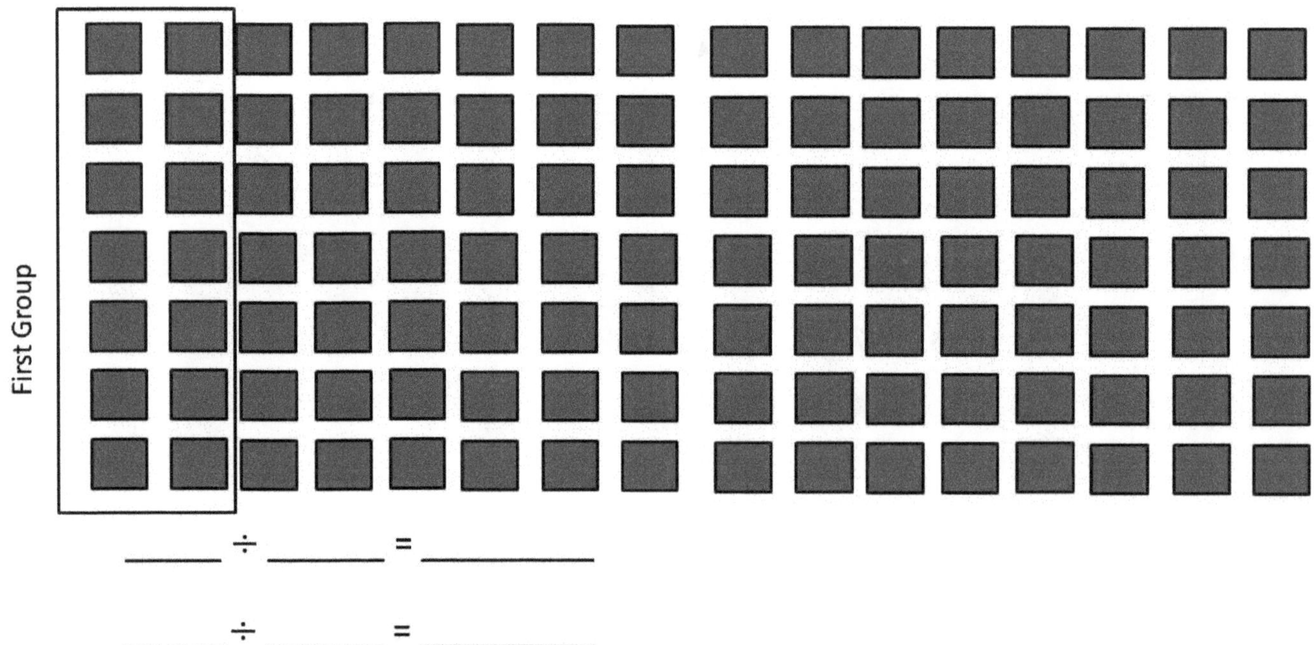

_____ ÷ _____ = _____

_____ ÷ _____ = _____

13: While dividing cakes amongst her friends Nikitha observed that all her 30 friends received 4 cakes each and there was three cakes extra for herself including her own share. Find total cakes with which she started distribution.

Worksheet 4

A: Complete the following.

1. 5 × 2 × 7 _____

2. 8 × 3 × 2 _____

3. 4 × 2 × 5 _____

4. 5 × 3 × 4 _____

5. 6 × 3 × 1 _____

6. 4 × 2 × 4 _____

13. 4 × ☐ × 8 = 64 _____

14. 2 × 4 × ☐ = 80 _____

15. 4 × ☐ × 5 = 60 _____

7. 7 × 2 × 6 _____

8. 9 × 4 × 2 _____

9. 10 × 12 × 1 _____

10. 6 × 2 × 5 _____

11. 5 × 4 × 2 _____

12. 0 × 12 × 1 _____

17. 5 × 3 × 4 = ☐ _____

18. 10 × 11 × ☐ = 0 _____

19. 5 × 1 × 4 = ☐ _____

B: Find outer boundary.

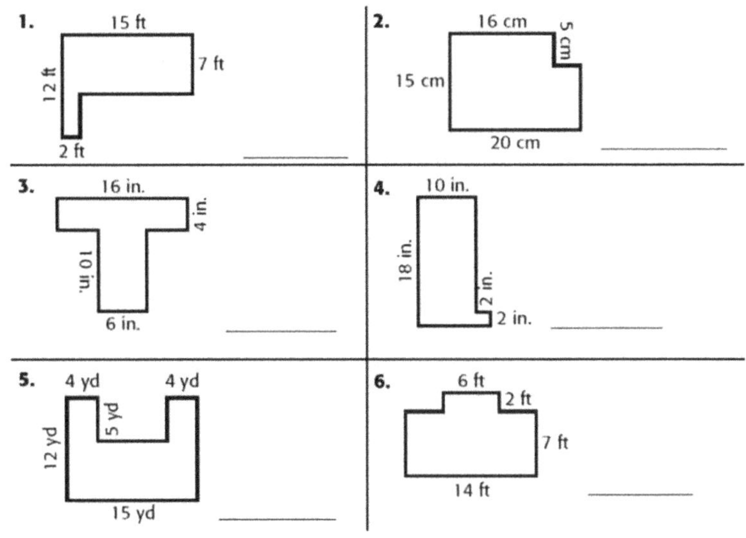

6. Find outer boundary of the following shape. Each square in this shape are of equal sides.

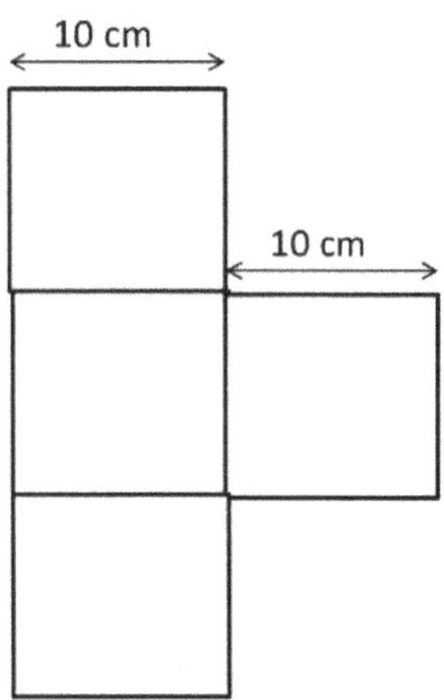

Worksheet 5

A: Complete the following.

1. 29 + 39 = ____	1. 624 - 84 = ____	1. 80 x 30 = ____	1. 240 ÷ 80 = ____
2. 86 + 42 = ____	2. 120 - 65 = ____	2. 50 x 90 = ____	2. 280 ÷ 70 = ____
3. 94 + 194 = ____	3. 358 - 126 = ____	3. 70 x 70 = ____	3. 540 ÷ 60 = ____
4. 231 + 79 = ____	4. 836 - 95 = ____	4. 60 x 80 = ____	4. 480 ÷ 40 = ____
5. 412 + 130 = ____	5. 312 - 105 = ____	5. 90 x 80 = ____	5. 250 ÷ 50 = ____
6. 351 + 251 = ____	6. 87 - 32 = ____	6. 300 x 60 = ____	6. 360 ÷ 6 = ____
7. 99 + 121 = ____	7. 169 - 48 = ____	7. 700 x 50 = ____	7. 180 ÷ 3 = ____
8. 517 + 217 = ____	8. 254 - 89 = ____	8. 60 x 700 = ____	8. 960 ÷ 12 = ____
9. 813 + 99 = ____	9. 96 - 45 = ____	9. 40 x 900 = ____	9. 200 ÷ 4 = ____
10. 275 + 75 = ____	10. 326 - 83 = ____	10. 20 x 600 = ____	10. 240 ÷ 12 = ___

B: Find area of the following figures in unit area.

1  2  3 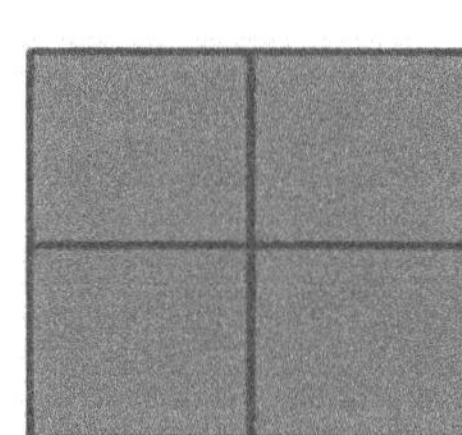 4 

5 a  5 b  5 c 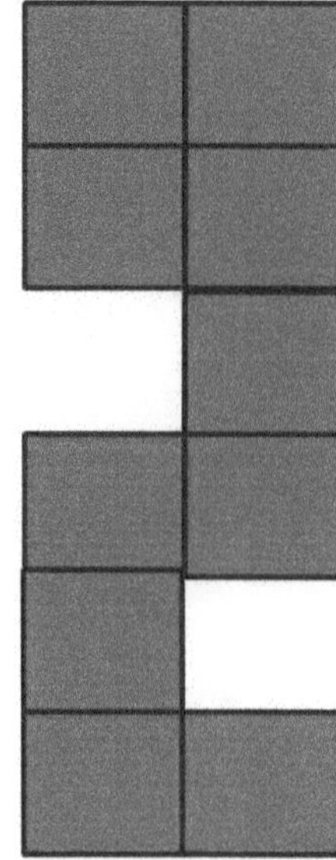 6 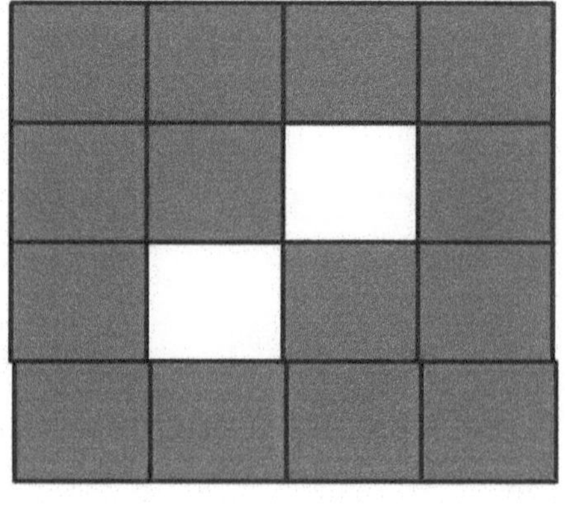

7. 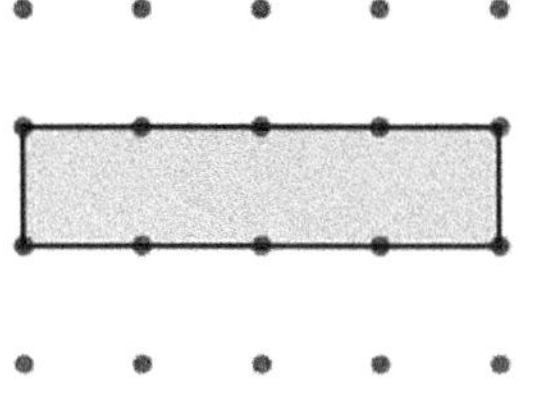

8. 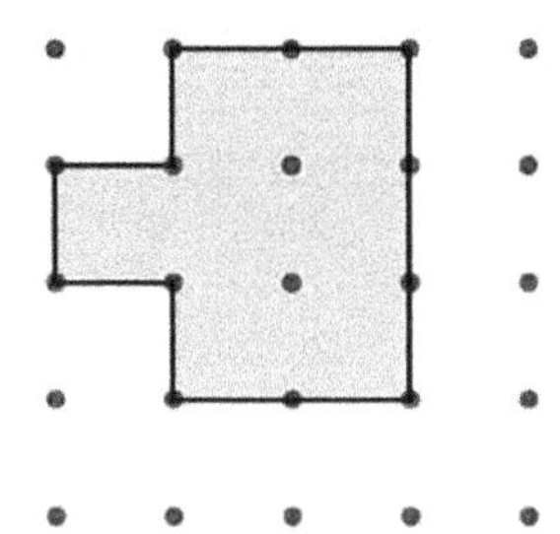

9. 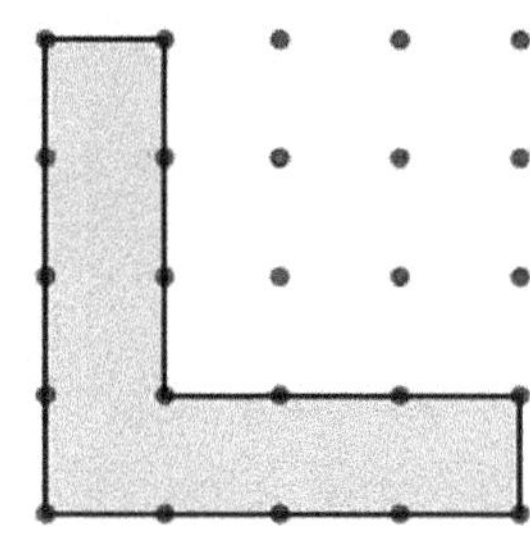

Area = _____ square units

Area = _____ square units

Area = _____ square units

10. 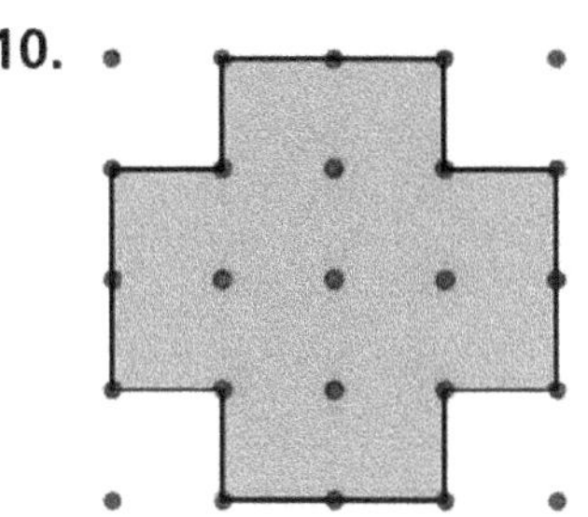

11. 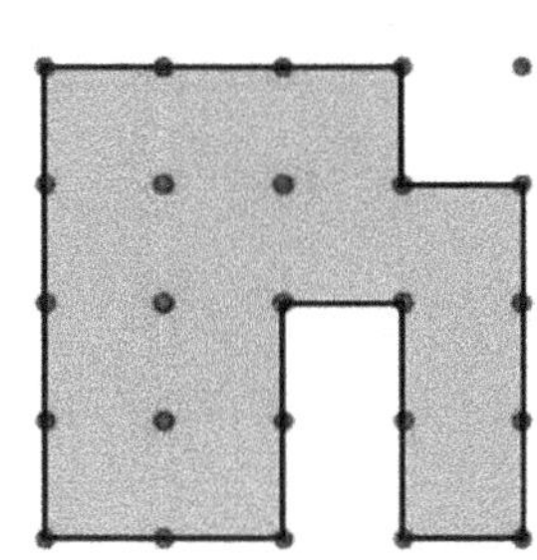

12. 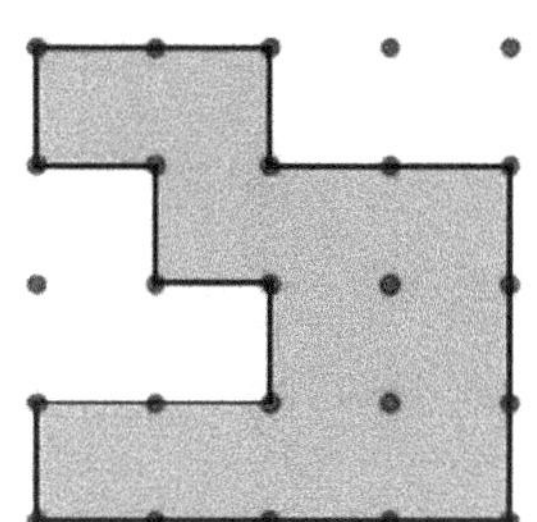

C: Find areas.

1. Calculate area of the following combination of squares arranged in a definite pattern. Each of the square is of side 10 cm

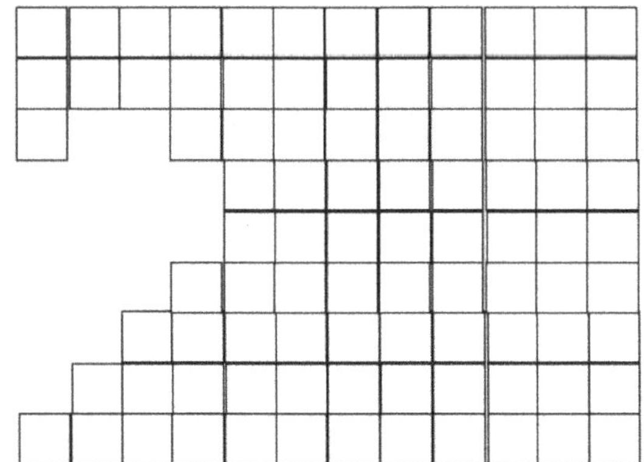

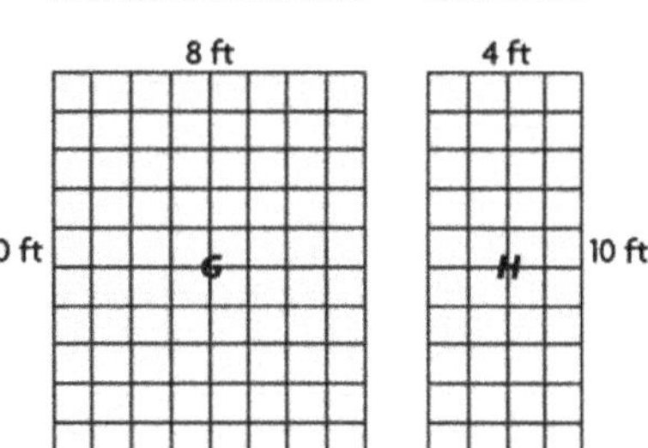

Area of a square can be calculated by multiplying valuse of two sides.

Side of a square = side X side = ____ cm X ____ cm

= ____ square cm.

2. Compare the areas of figure E, F , G and H and arrange the values in ascending order.

Worksheet 6

A: Division.

1. $6\overline{)56}$ _______

2. $5\overline{)42}$ _______

3. $6\overline{)25}$ _______

4. $2\overline{)32}$ _______

5. $5\overline{)41}$ _______

6. $9\overline{)53}$ _______

7. $6\overline{)54}$ ___

8. $6\overline{)34}$ _______

9. $8\overline{)21}$ _______

10. $7\overline{)35}$ ___

11. $72 \div 8$ _______

12. $15 \div 7$ _______

13. $64 \div 7$ _______

14. $49 \div 3$ _______

15. $28 \div 3$ _______

17. Write division sentence

_______ $\div$ _______ $=$ _________

16. Nikita got 7 whole and a half slice of apples to be shared along with her six intimate friends who joined the party. Each of her fellow friends will get _______ apple(s).

B: Column matchning.

Column A	Column B
1. closed shape •	• A part of a line that includes two endpoints and all the points between them
2. line segment •	• A shape formed by two rays that share an endpoint
3. right angle •	• A shape that starts and ends at the same point
4. hexagon •	• An angle that forms a square corner
5. angle •	• A closed plane shape made up of line segments
6. polygon •	• A polygon with 6 sides and 6 angles

line
line segment
open shape
parallel lines
perpendicular lines
point
polygon
✓ quadrilateral
ray
✓ rectangle
✓ rhombus
right angle
✓ square
✓ trapezoid
✓ triangle

Worksheet 7

1. 6)‾300‾ ______

2. 5)‾2,000‾ ______

3. 4)‾3,600‾ ______

4. 2)‾1,000‾ ______

5. 6)‾1,200‾ ______

6. 5)‾1,000‾ ______

7. 2)‾1,800‾ ______

8. 8)‾4,000‾ ______

9. 9)‾2,700‾ ______

10. 8)‾3,200‾ ______

11. 4)‾4,000‾ ______

12. 3)‾2,100‾ ______

13. 5)‾3,500‾ ______

14. 6)‾2,400‾ ______

15. 7)‾2,800‾ ______

16: Provide correct options.

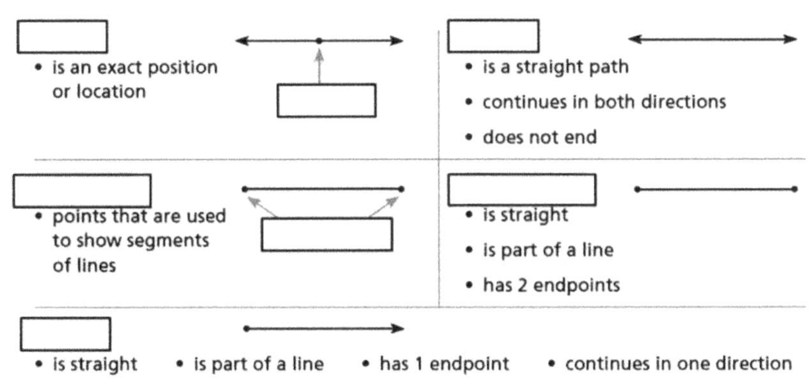

Options: Ray, Endpoint, point, line segment, line,

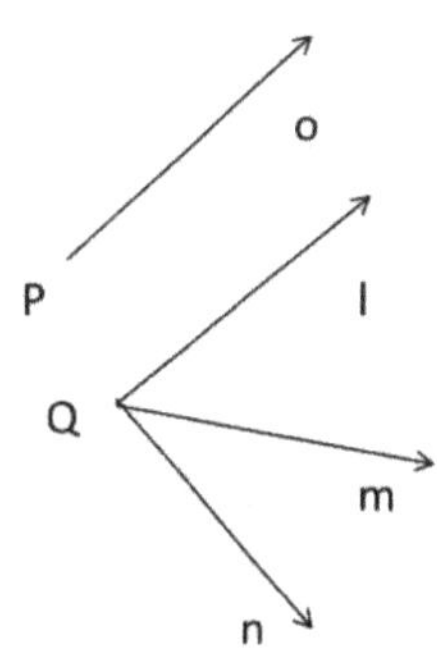

Ray _____, _____ and _______ have a common origin. Ray ____ is not sharing any common point with ray l or m.

17: Rijuana prefers painting on a rectangular papers, Pomelia prefers Square sized apers and Nomithalina refers pentagonal papers for that activity. Circular papers are there there for Groseliana. Which of the above mentioned shape is not a polygon?

18. _________ line(s) can be drawn passing through three given points.

19. ________ have only one end point and can be extended endlessly in any one direction.

20. _______ have no end points and can be extended endlessly in both the directions.

21. Points not lying on any straight line are called collinear points. ________ lines can be drawn by taking any two out of three non-collinear points.

22. Observe the diagram in which students are arranged in a pattern.

Write two number sentences to represent the total number of students doing Yoga.

_______X_______ = _______; ________ X ________ = _______

If we arrange them in 9 columns then number of rows will be ________.

***.

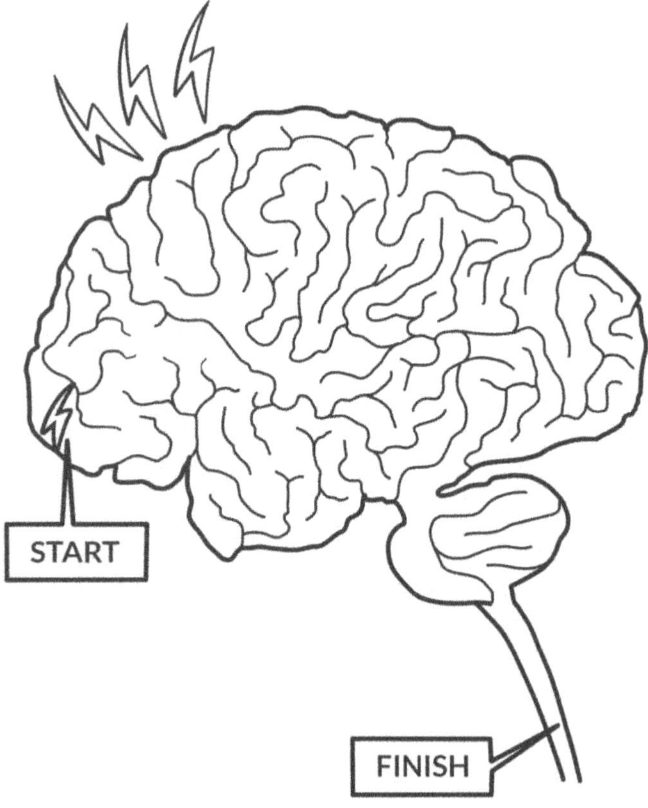

Worksheet 8

I: Perform the following basic oeprations: ---

1. 8)242 _______ **2.** 8)641 _______

3. 5)402 _______ **4.** 6)241 _______

5. 7)563 _______ **6.** 4)121 _______

7. 3)273 _______ **8.** 5)149 _______

9. 8)161 _______ **10.** 7)494 _______

11. 9)184 _______ **12.** 9)629 _______

13. 3)301 _______ **14.** 9)453 _______

15. 6)331 _______ **16.** 2)804 _______

17. 6)422 _______ **18.** 5)247 _______

19. 9)625 _______ **20.** 8)639 _______

21. Write division sentence

_______ ÷ _______ = _______

II: Complete the following.

1.

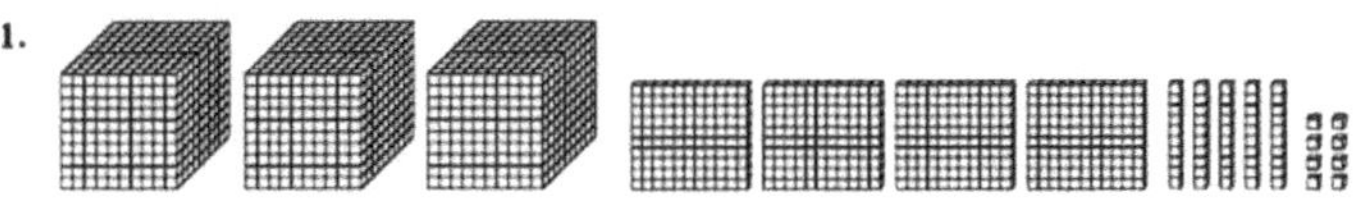

____

2. 8,000 + 600 + 20 + 1

____

3. 2,000 + 400 + 20 + 9

____

4. 3,000 + 500 + 7

____

5. 1,000 + 900 + 80 + 2

____

Write in expanded form.

6. 5,083

____

7. 6,493

____

9. Expand the following.

5,462 = _______ + _______ + _____ + _____

8.914 = _______ + _______ + _____ + _____

4,075 = _______ + _______ + _____ + _____

4,705 = _______ + _______ + _____ + _____

9,504 = _______ + _______ + _____ + _____

5,050 = _______ + _______ + _____ + _____

7,069 = _______ + _______ + _____ + _____

2,435 = _______ + _______ + _____ + _____

8. Pandelonica added 71 hundreds , 29 hundreds to the smallest number of five digits. Find the digit which will be there at thousands and hundreds place of the result.

III: Somalenia took 400 beads to arrange them in such a way that there should be 8 columns. Find the number of rows in that arrangement.

Worksheet 9

1. 21 ÷ 4 ________

2. 89 ÷ 6 ________

3. 170 ÷ 3 ________

4. 442 ÷ 5 ________

5. 712 ÷ 8 _____

6. 145 ÷ 3 ________

7. 165 ÷ 9 ________

8. 368 ÷ 7 ________

9. 125 ÷ 7 ________

11. 324 ÷ 9 ______

12. 364 ÷ 7 _____

13. 498 ÷ 5 ______

14. 642 ÷ 7 ______

15. 432 ÷ 8 _____

16. 681 ÷ 7 _____

17. 251 ÷ 8 _____

18. 219 ÷ 7 _____

19. 868 ÷ 9 _____

21. Write division sentence

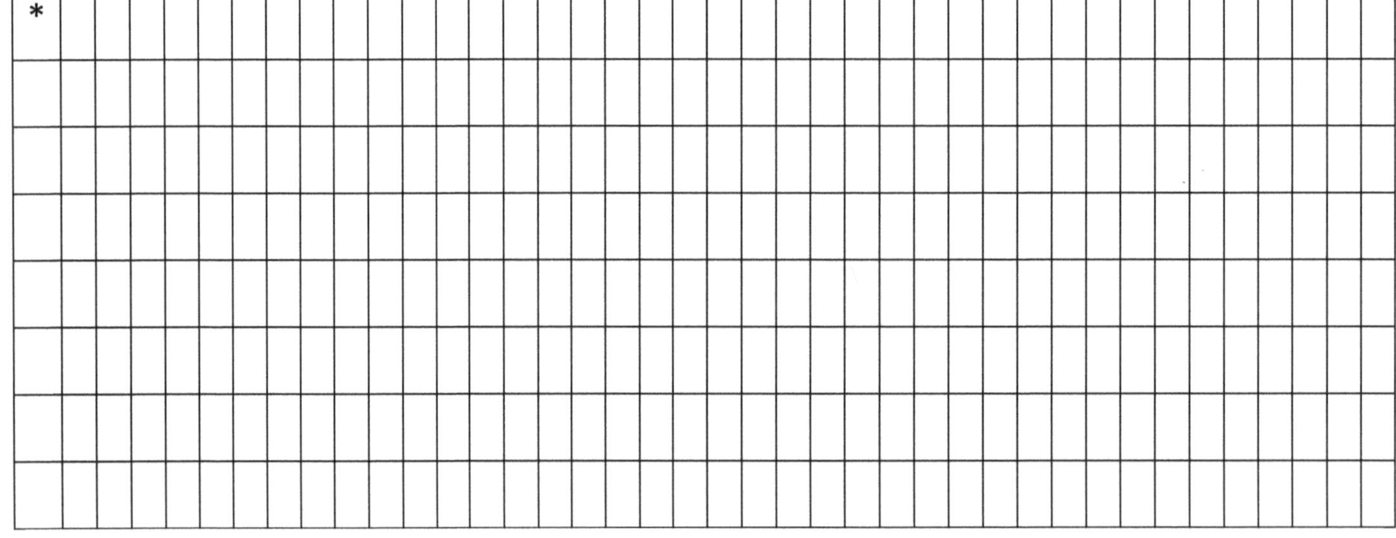

______ ÷ ______ = ________

20. Panteloneria collected 12 cards from each of her fellow friends and her collection of all such cards were arranged in the collection folder in which there is 24 pages comprising 10 cards in each page. Find the number of card contributors.

22. Write division sentences for the following grid.

23: Complete the following Number chart.

Numbers	Periods and Places								
	Millions			Thousands			Ones		
	Hundred Millions	Ten Millions	Millions	Hundred Thousands	Ten Thousands	Thousands	Hundreds	Tens	Ones
132,324,432				3					
505,506,507	5								
345,435,543							5		
433,434,433				4					
101,101,101	1								
21,211,232		2	1						
202,305,765									

24: A ropeway has markings at an equal interval of 2m. Such marking is absent at the beginning and at the end. Find total number of such markings in a 260 m long rope.

25: A glass contains 100 ml milk. A container holds 5 l water. That glass is used to fill up the water container. Find the total number of times that glass is used to fill up the water container. [1 l = 1,000 ml]

26: Write in standard form and find the digit present at hundreds place.

32 thousands + 43 hundreds + 21 tens + 43 tens + 65 ones = ______________.

Worksheet 10

1. 5)5,098

2. 6)6,485

3. 2)$3,458

4. 6)7,349

5. 7)8,655

6. 5)5,437

7. 9)$9,950

10. 2)8,642

11. 3)$4,743

12. 5)$8,115

13. 3)83,765

14. 2)60,567

15. 4)84,219

16. 3)98,651

17. Write division sentence

_______ ÷ _______ = _______

18. Somalia started dividing a three digit number by 4 and there was a remainder 3. If we add 5 to that number then the number will become a four digit number and also becone divisible by 4. Find the number.

19: Half of a number is equal to 2 more than the greatest three digit number. Find the number.

20: Instead to adding 100 Nikitha subtracted 100 from the given number and her resul was 4067. Santenalia corrected the sum and pointed out the original answer. Find the original answer.

21. $32 + 44 + 81 =$ _______

22. $56 + 14 + 39 =$ _______

23. $82 + 8 + 18 =$ _______

24. $28 + 27 + 42 =$ _______

25. $4{,}290 - 3{,}735 =$ _______

26. $10{,}802 - 6{,}529 =$ _______

27. $5{,}000 - 655 =$ _______

28. $3{,}800 - 799 =$ _______

29: Data representing number of girl students in different classes.

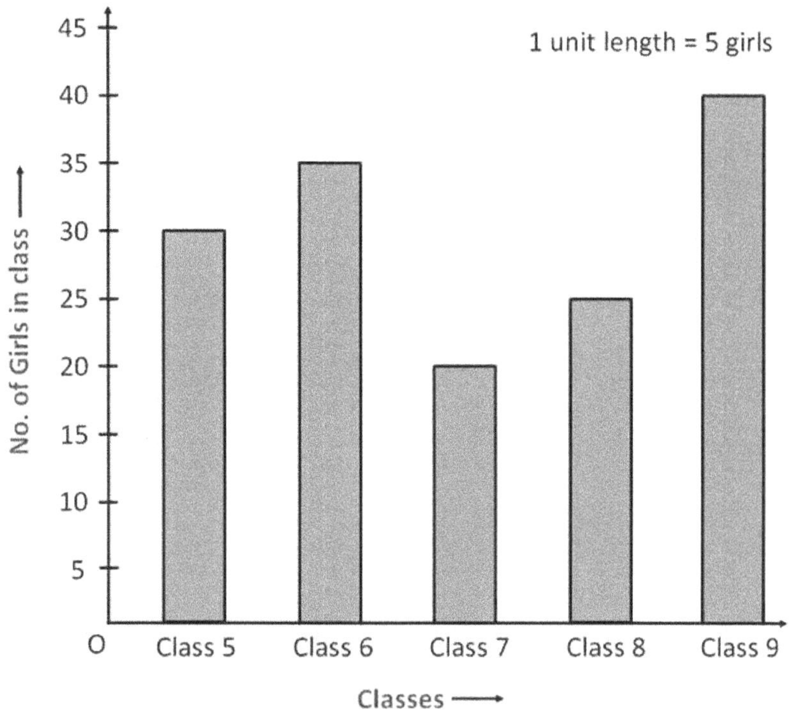

Number of girls in class 9 is ____________ than the total number of girls in class 5 and 6. The difference of the strngth in class 6 and 7 is ____________. Average number of girls in all the classes from 5th to 9th is ______________ . it is ___________________ _____________ than the strength of class 9.

30: Bill and Mark prepared two different patterns by using square sized papers of side 10 cm each. They individually used 100 such strips. Bill arranged them in a linear fashion. Mark arranged them to obtain a large square. Find the perimeter recorded by both the fellow partner. Compare both the values.

31: A train covers distance equal to its own length whil crossing a passenger standing on platform. An express train was moving with a speed of 10 m per second. That train will cover 10 m distance in a second and took 50 seconds to cross the passenger standing on platform. Find length of that train.

Worksheet 11

I: Identify following polygons and write their names.

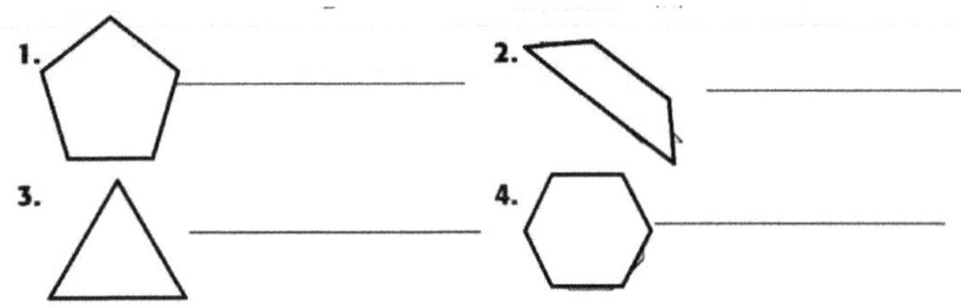

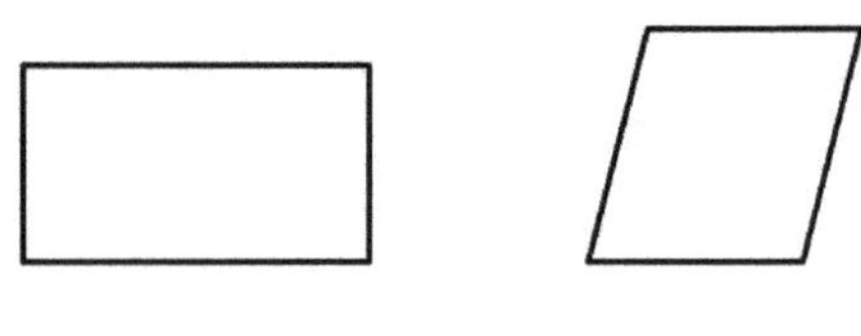

9. Identify things common in all the following shaes.

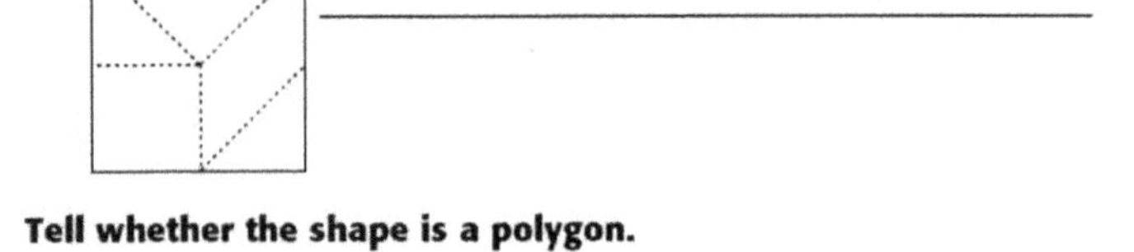

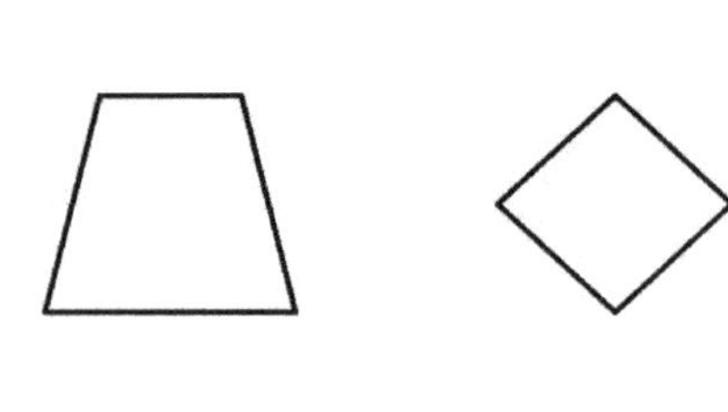

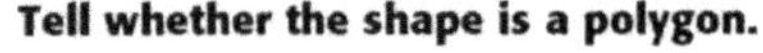

Tell whether the shape is a polygon.

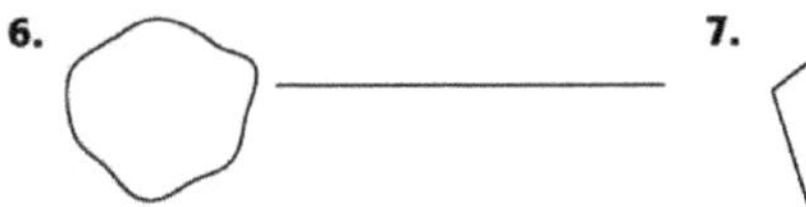

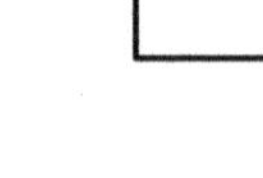

8. Complete the pattern ...

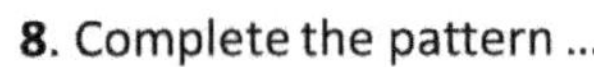

II: Rays and lines.

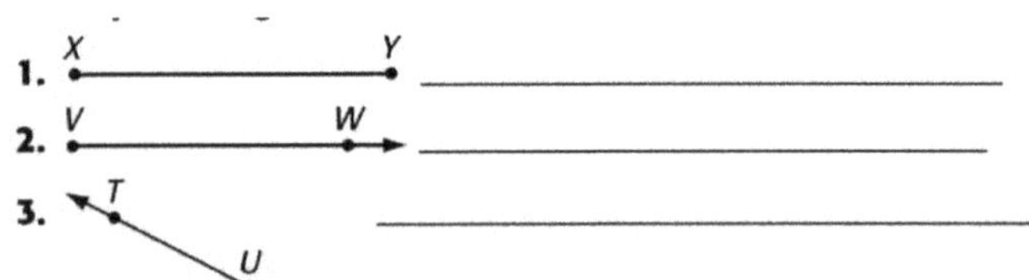

9. Identify three line segments from the following figure.

Describe the figure.

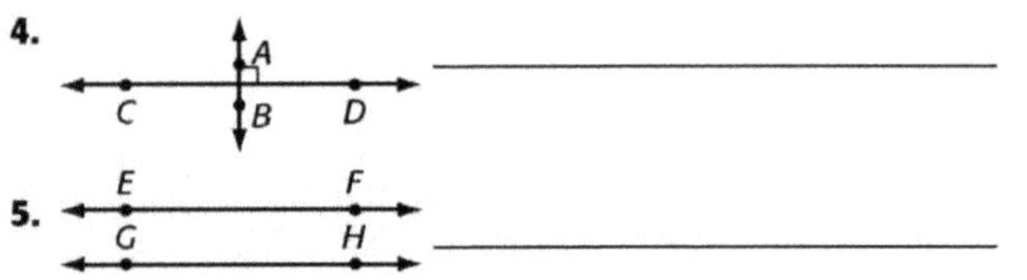

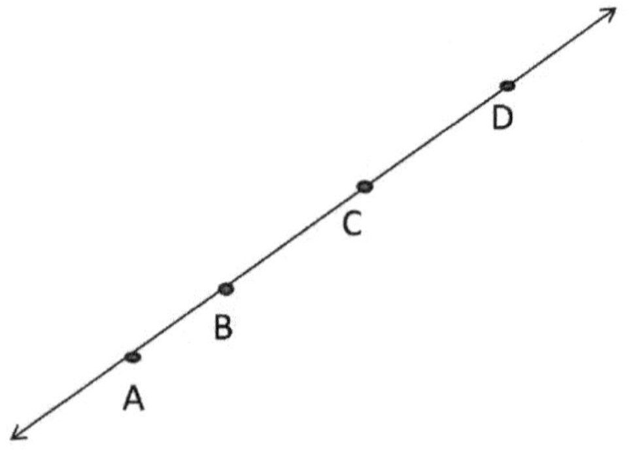

Draw an example of each.

7. ray *CD*

8. line segment *FG*

III: Calculate Perimeter (Outer boundaries).

7.
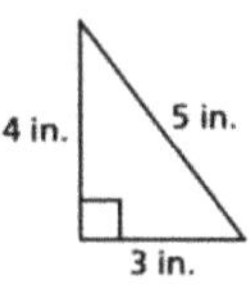

8.
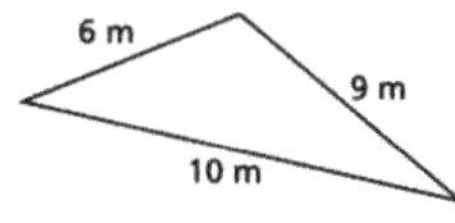

14. Find and compare outer boundary of the following shapes. Both the shapes are made u of identical units of squares of side 5 cm each.

____

9.
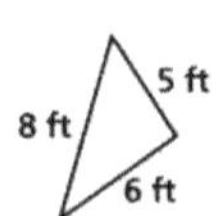

10.
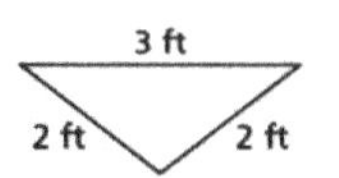

____

11.
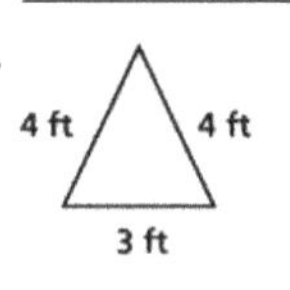

12.
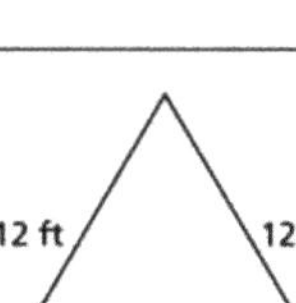

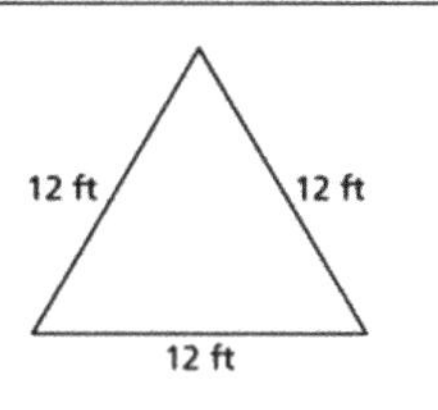

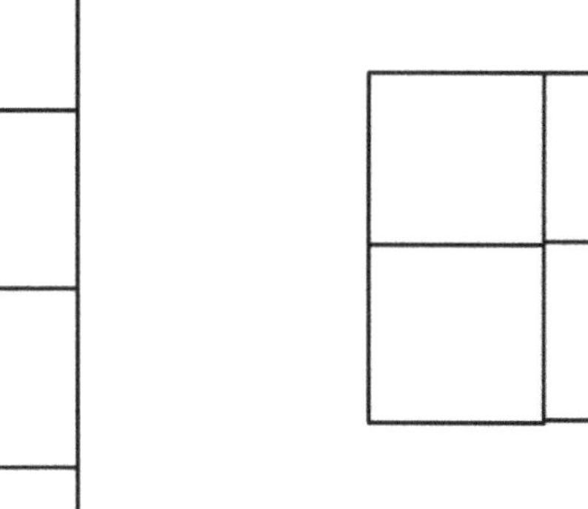

____

IV: Answer the following.

1. Ten Million = ____________________ thousand.

2. ________________ Hundred thousand = 212 million.

3. 432 thousand = ____________ tens.

4. Predecessor of 6 digit greatest number = _____ million.

5. Successor of a three digit smallest even number = ____________.

6. What number must be subtracted from 10 million to make it greatest six digit number?

7. 10,101 X ____________________ = 91,000 − 91.

8. Place value of 4 in 132,435,435 is ____________________.

9. Sum total of place values of 5 in the following numbers = ____________________.

10.   325,435,329; 405,435,403   and 105,404,321

11. Arrange the following numbers in ascending order.

12.   213,435,647; 544,432,123 and 324,324,546

13. What least number must be added to make 1023987 divisible by 4 and also divisible by 3?

14. Is there any Natural Number having no predecessor?.

Worksheet 12

I: Complete the numeration table.

Numbers	Periods and Places								
	Crores		Lakhs		Thousands		Ones		
	Ten Crores	Crores	Ten Lakhs	Lakhs	Ten Thousands	Thousands	Hundreds	Tens	Ones
21,32,43,654									
20,03,43,031	2							3	1
43,65,87,087		3							
32,43,76,980									0
20,20,43,203		0		0		3	2		
43,75,65,765									
10,10,10,101									
90,98,90,980									
43,43,540									
32,50,045									

II: In how many different ways the number 16 can be represented in the form of product of its factors?

[Example: 16 = 1 X 2 X 8; 16 = 1 X 4 X 4; explore other such ways.]

III: Divisor is a number which can divide another number. That divisor will be a perfect divisor if remainders are not obtained. Find at least one common divisor for the following set of numbers.

Worksheet 13

Expanded form of numeration:

Expansion in International Numeration

211,321,213 =   200,000,000 + 10,000,000 + 1,000,000 + 300,000   + 20,000 + 1,000 + 200 + 10 + 3

1. Complete the following:

a. 321,403,320 =

b. 324,432,543   = ___ X 100,000,000

+ ____X 10,000,000

+ ____X 1,000,000

+ ____X 100,000

+ ____X 10,000

+ ____X 1,000

+ ____X 100

+ ____X 10

+ ____X 1

c. 203,304,405 =

d. 213,323,323 =

e. Write a number greater than 50,000 by using digits 5, 4 and 2.

f. 403 thousands = __________________ tens.

g. 32 million = ___________ thousands.

h. ___________ million is 200 greater than 9,999,800.

i. Write a number smaller than 39 million by using digits 4, 3 and 8. Digits can be repeated.

j. Even numbers have digits 0.2.4.6 or 8 at ones position. What least number should be subtracted from the greatest three digit number to obtain a greatest even number of three digits?

k. Sum total of any two odd number will be an ___________ number only.

Worksheet 14

I: Complete the following place value chart.

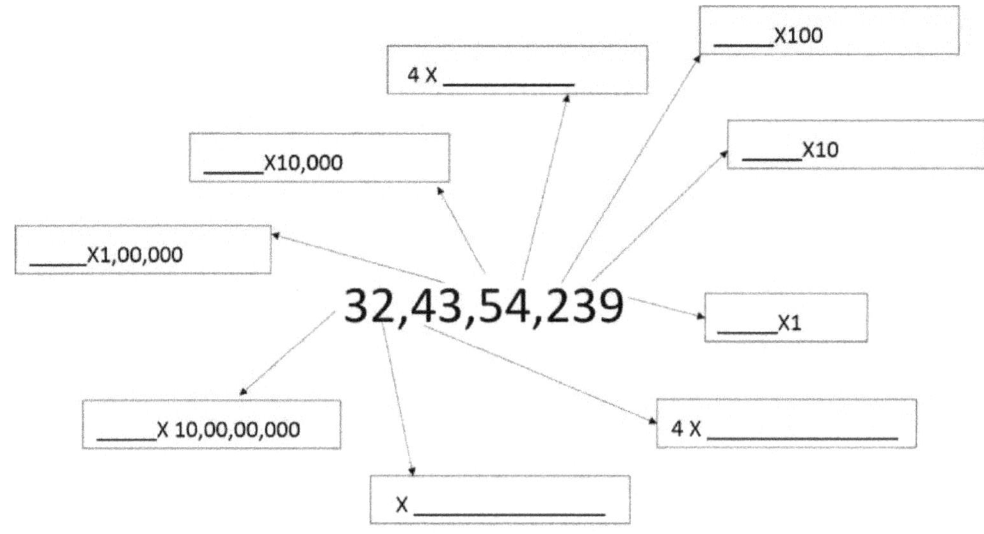

II: Solve the following.

2. $\begin{array}{r}9\\ \times 5\\\hline\end{array}$	3. $\begin{array}{r}10\\ \times 9\\\hline\end{array}$	4. $\begin{array}{r}10\\ \times 6\\\hline\end{array}$	5. $\begin{array}{r}10\\ \times 8\\\hline\end{array}$	6. $\begin{array}{r}9\\ \times 4\\\hline\end{array}$
7. $\begin{array}{r}9\\ \times 6\\\hline\end{array}$	8. $\begin{array}{r}10\\ \times 5\\\hline\end{array}$	9. $\begin{array}{r}10\\ \times 3\\\hline\end{array}$	10. $\begin{array}{r}7\\ \times 9\\\hline\end{array}$	11. $\begin{array}{r}10\\ \times 2\\\hline\end{array}$
12. $\begin{array}{r}9\\ \times 3\\\hline\end{array}$	13. $\begin{array}{r}10\\ \times 4\\\hline\end{array}$	14. $\begin{array}{r}9\\ \times 9\\\hline\end{array}$	15. $\begin{array}{r}10\\ \times 7\\\hline\end{array}$	16. $\begin{array}{r}8\\ \times 9\\\hline\end{array}$

17. $8 \times 10 =$ _____   18. $9 \times 2 =$ _____   19. $1 \times 10 =$ _____

20. $1 \times 9 =$ _____   21. $9 \times 10 =$ _____   22. $9 \times 5 =$ _____

23. $10 \times 2 =$ _____   24. $10 \times 8 =$ _____   25. $9 \times 7 =$ _____

Find the missing factor.

26. $\square \times 8 = 0$ 27. $\square \times 2 = 20$ 28. $7 \times \square = 7$

29. $9 \times \square = 6 \times 3$ 30. $5 \times 8 = \square \times 10$ 31. $\square \times 9 = 6 \times 6$

Worksheet 15

1. Numbers divisible by 2 are also called __________ numbers.

2. ____ is the only even prime number.

3. All prime numbers have only _____ factors. ____ and the number itself.

4. Sum total of 2 eve numbers is always an ________ number.

5. Sum total of an even number and an odd number is always an _____ number.

6. A prime number between 95 and 100 = __________.

7. All the multiples of 8 are also multiples of 2 and _______.

8. All the multiples of _____ and 4 may or may not be a multiple of 8.

9. All the multiples of ___ and _____ are not necessarily multiples of 10.

10. All multiples of 10 are also multiples of ______ and ______.

11. Four electric lights are turned on at the same time. First one blinks every 4 seconds, second one blinks every 6 seconds, third one blinks every 8 seconds and the fourth one blinks every 12 seconds. In 60 seconds, how many times will they blink at the same time?

12. Every 2nd, 5th and 10th visitor of a shopping complex receives gifts. How often do three visitors at a time will receive gifts?

13. Before last Saturday there was a rain. Weather station speculated advent of another rain after a couple of fortnight. Which of the forthcoming day would be a rainy day?

14. A circular ring was reshaped to design a square of side 39 cm. what was the circumference of the ring?

15. Rosenvansky added 250 to a given number and his result exceeded the four digit smallest number by 50. Find the number which was given to him.

16. Expand: 23,43,509 = __________ + _________ + ________+ _____+ ___ + ___+___

Worksheet 16

Expand the following

1: 32,404   2: 30,304   3: 30,30,909

Do as directed

4. Subtract :

i.   13 million – 123 thousands

ii.   103 thousands – 1,230

iii.   3,123,324 – 343 thousands

iv.   43,546,433 – 12,324,323

v.   21 million – 121,213

vi.   43 million – 123 hundreds

5. Subtract :

i.   104 million – 104 thousands

ii.   324 million – 5,463 thousands

iii.   213 lakhs– 1,023 thousands

iv.   93 lakhs – 423 thousands

v.   213,435,322– 101,101,101

vi.   40,05,605– 10,70,802

6. Multiply :

i.   213X 20,000 X10

ii.   10303X 400

iii.   101 X 100 X 200

iv.   50 X 50 X 500

v.   12,543 X 105

vi.   104 X 400 X 200

vii. 90 X 90 X 90

7. If 36 X 121 = 4,356 , then :

i.   36X10 X 100 =

ii.   36X 400 =

iii.   36 X 200 =

iv.   36 X 1,000 =

v.   4,356 ÷ 121 =

vi.   4,356 ÷ 36 =

vii. 4,356 ÷ 18 =

8. Observe the following :

$$1 + 2 + 3 + \ldots + 100 = 5,050$$

Now find the value :   2+ 4 + 6 + …. + 200 = ____________

Worksheet 17

I: Identify and write their names.

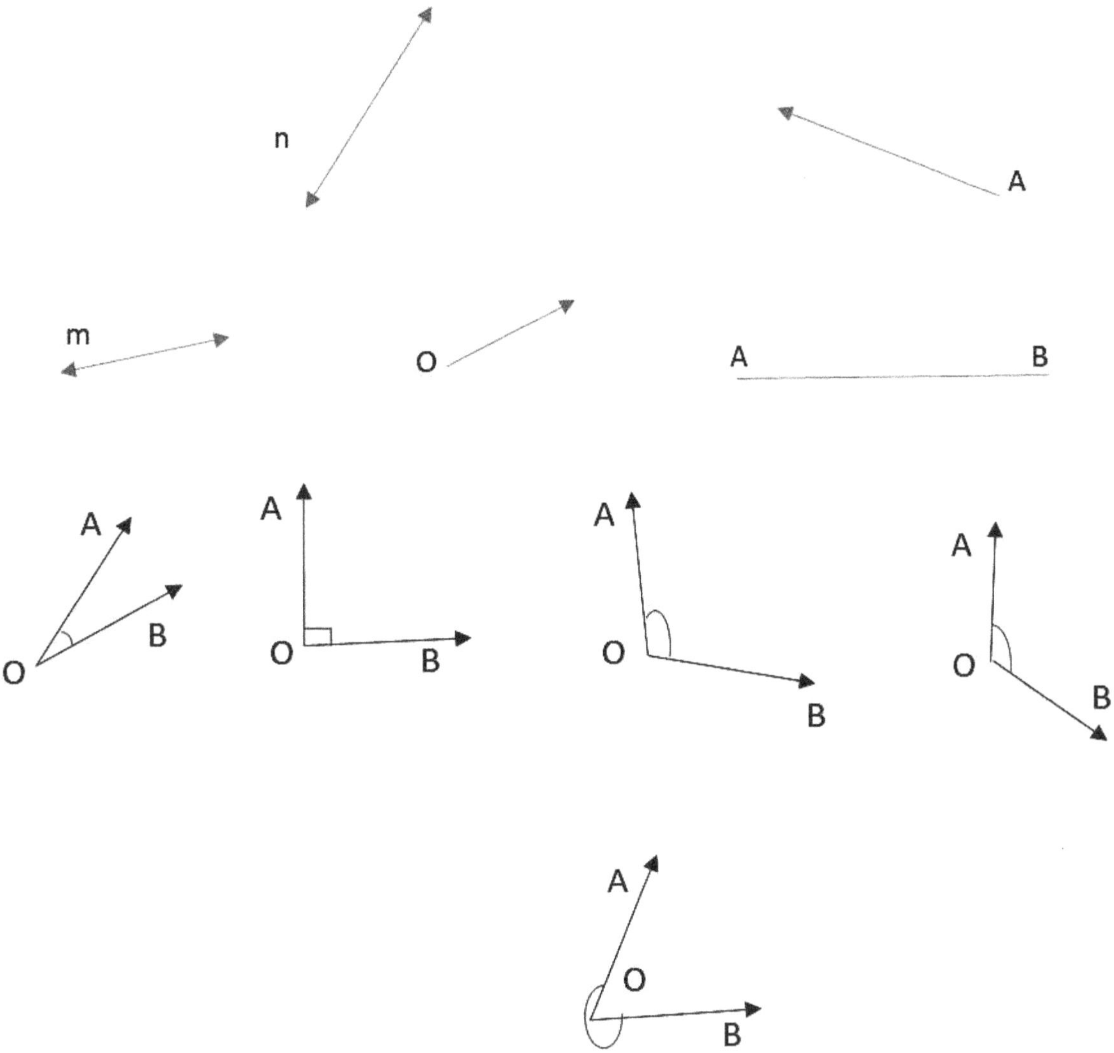

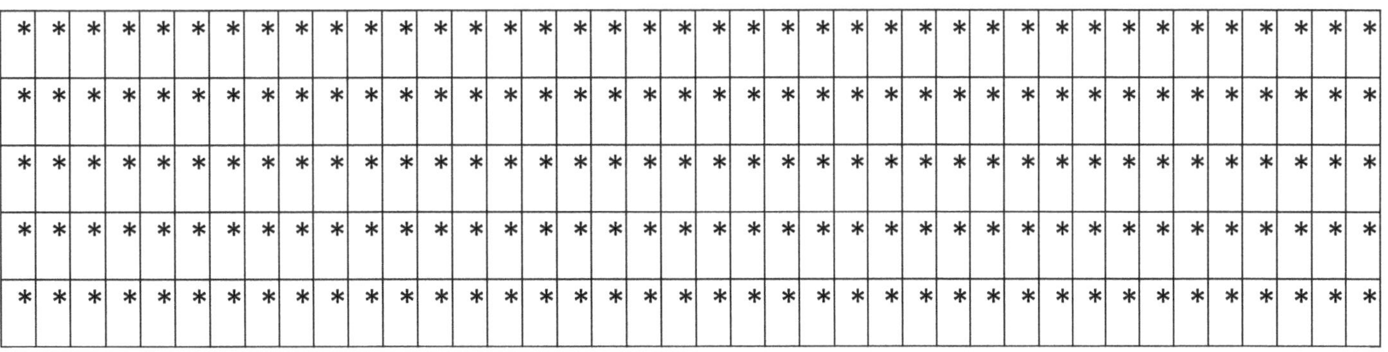

II: Write a number sentence to represent the following grid.

*	*	*	*	*	*	*	*	*	*	*	*	*	*	*	*	*	*	*	*	*	*	*	*	*	*	*	*	*	*	*	*	*	*	*	*	*	*	*	*
*	*	*	*	*	*	*	*	*	*	*	*	*	*	*	*	*	*	*	*	*	*	*	*	*	*	*	*	*	*	*	*	*	*	*	*	*	*	*	*
*	*	*	*	*	*	*	*	*	*	*	*	*	*	*	*	*	*	*	*	*	*	*	*	*	*	*	*	*	*	*	*	*	*	*	*	*	*	*	*
*	*	*	*	*	*	*	*	*	*	*	*	*	*	*	*	*	*	*	*	*	*	*	*	*	*	*	*	*	*	*	*	*	*	*	*	*	*	*	*
*	*	*	*	*	*	*	*	*	*	*	*	*	*	*	*	*	*	*	*	*	*	*	*	*	*	*	*	*	*	*	*	*	*	*	*	*	*	*	*

III: Cmplete the following.

1. $(3 \times 2) \times 3 =$ _____   2. $6 \times (4 \times 2) =$ _____   3. $(3 \times 3) \times 5 =$ _____

4. $(2 \times 2) \times 8 =$ _____   5. $(1 \times 4) \times 7 =$ _____   6. $4 \times (7 \times 1) =$ _____

7. $6 \times (0 \times 7) =$ _____   8. $(3 \times 3) \times 10 =$ _____   9. $(7 \times 1) \times 8 =$ _____

Use the Grouping Property to find the product.

10. $3 \times 3 \times 6 =$ _____   11. $4 \times 4 \times 2 =$ _____   12. $9 \times 3 \times 2 =$ _____

13. $7 \times 2 \times 2 =$ _____   14. $(2 \times 4) \times 7 =$ _____   15. $4 \times (9 \times 1) =$ _____

16. $4 \times 2 \times 5 =$ _____   17. $(3 \times 2) \times 10 =$ _____   18. $4 \times 2 \times 7 =$ _____

Find the missing factor.

19. $(8 \times$ _____$) \times 8 = 0$ 20. _____ $\times (3 \times 2) = 36$ 21. $($_____ $\times 4) \times 3 = 12$

22. $6 \times (3 \times$ _____$) = 54$ 23. $(3 \times 3) \times$ _____ $= 90$ 24. _____ $\times (5 \times 2) = 80$

25. $($_____ $\times 1) \times 1 = 6$ 26. $4 \times ($_____ $\times 4) = 32$ 27. $(2 \times 4) \times$ _____ $= 64$

26. $(6 + 6 + 6 +$ .... $1,000$ times $) = 6 \times$ _________ $=$ ___________.

27. $4 \times 25 = 100; \quad 5 \times 20 = 100;$ Find value of the following:

$121 \times 25 \times 20 \times 4 \times 5 \quad = 121 \times$ _____ $\times$ _____ $\quad = 121 \times$ __________.

28. $19324 \times (200) = 19324 \times ($_____ $+$ _____$) = 19324 \times$ ______ $+ 19324 \times 50$

29. $(10 + 10 + 10 + 10 +$ .... 100 times $) = 10 \times$ ______ $=$ __ $\times 1,000$

30. $1897 +$ ______ $= 2,000$; Find the missing number.

31. Predecessor of three digit greatest even number $=$ _____________.

IV: Facti family.

We can write fact family for the group of number 8, 9 and 72 in different ways as follows:

72 = 8 X 9;   8 X 9 = 72;   72/9 = 8;   72/8 = 9;

Preapre fact family for the following:

1. 4, 9, 36   **2.** 8, 3, 24   **3.** 6, 4, 24

__________   __________   __________

__________   __________   __________

__________   __________   __________

__________   __________   __________

4. 6, 6, 36   **5.** 7, 7, 49   **6.** 5, 5, 25

__________   __________   __________

__________   __________   __________

Find the quotient or product.

7. $5 \times 7 =$ ____   **8.** $7 \times 5 =$ ____   **9.** $35 \div 7 =$ ____   **10.** $35 \div 5 =$ ____

Write the other three sentences in the fact family.

11. $6 \times 3 = 18$ **12.** $4 \times 5 = 20$ **13.** $2 \times 7 = 14$

Sbject Enrichment

1: Write the numbers –

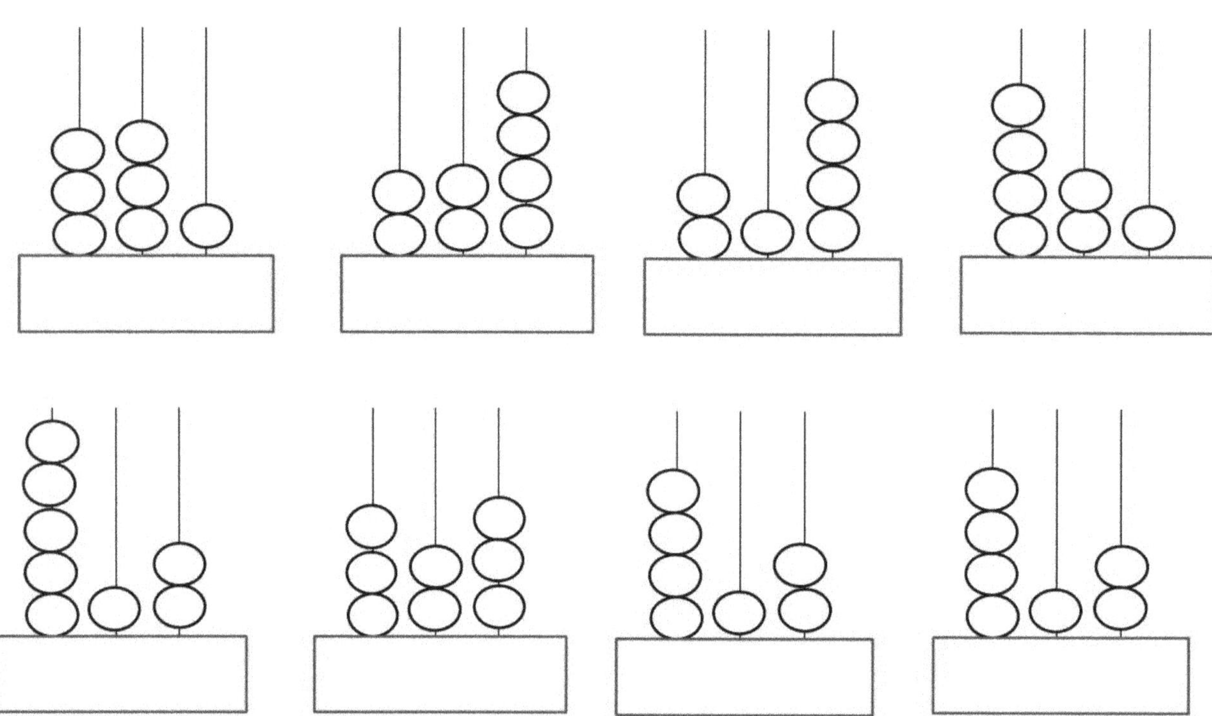

2: Make a number sentence to represent the following grid pattern.

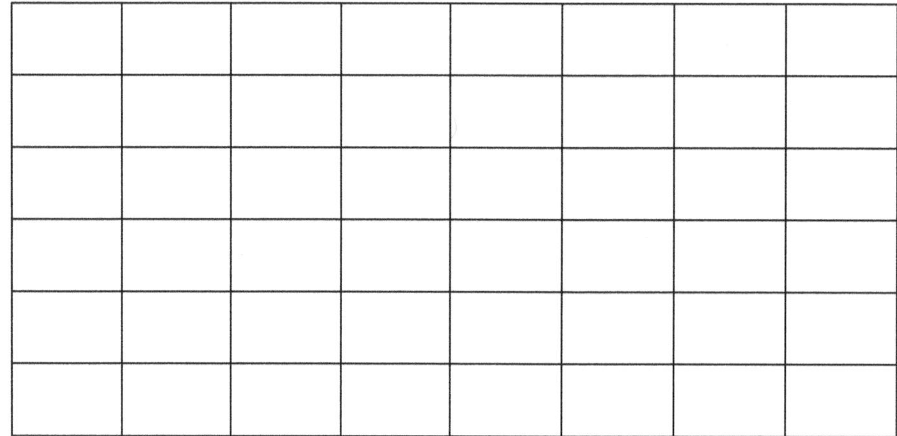

8 X _____ = _____;   6 X _____ = _____; 48 = ___ X _____;

9: Find missing numbers in the following pattern:

12				20				30

10: Record of Rainfall ----

		*			
		*			
*		*			
*	*	*			
*	*	*			
*	*	*			
*	*	*	*		
*	*	*	*		
*	*	*	*	*	
*	*	*	*	*	*
*	*	*	*	*	*
August	September	October	November	December	January

Maximum rainfall recorded during ___________.

There was negligible rainfall in ___________.

Total rainfall during November to January was not exceeding the rainfall recorded during _______________.

Maximum number of rainy day recorded during ___________ followed by _____________.

11: Join dots as per numbers given

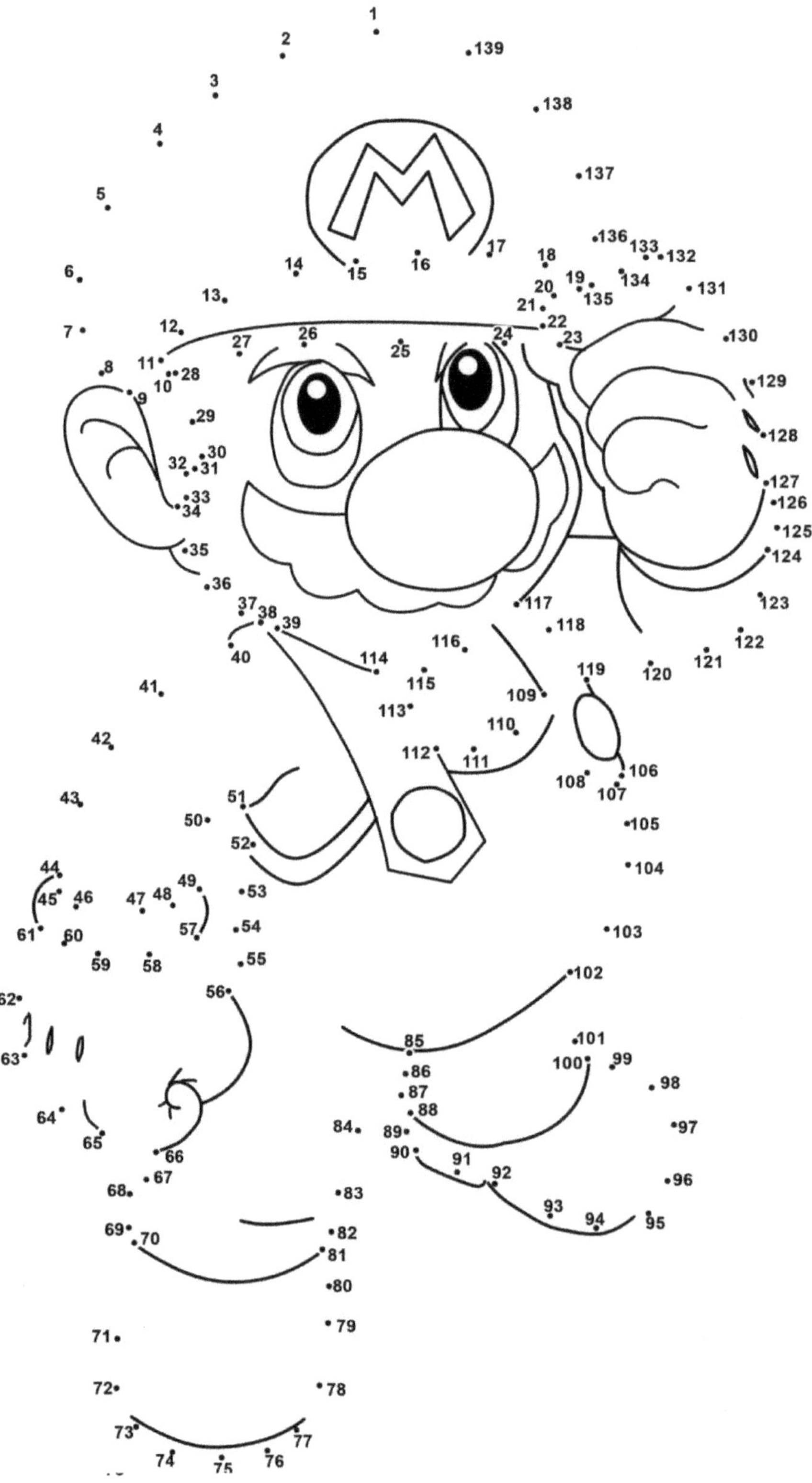

12: Join dots and identify basic shapes.

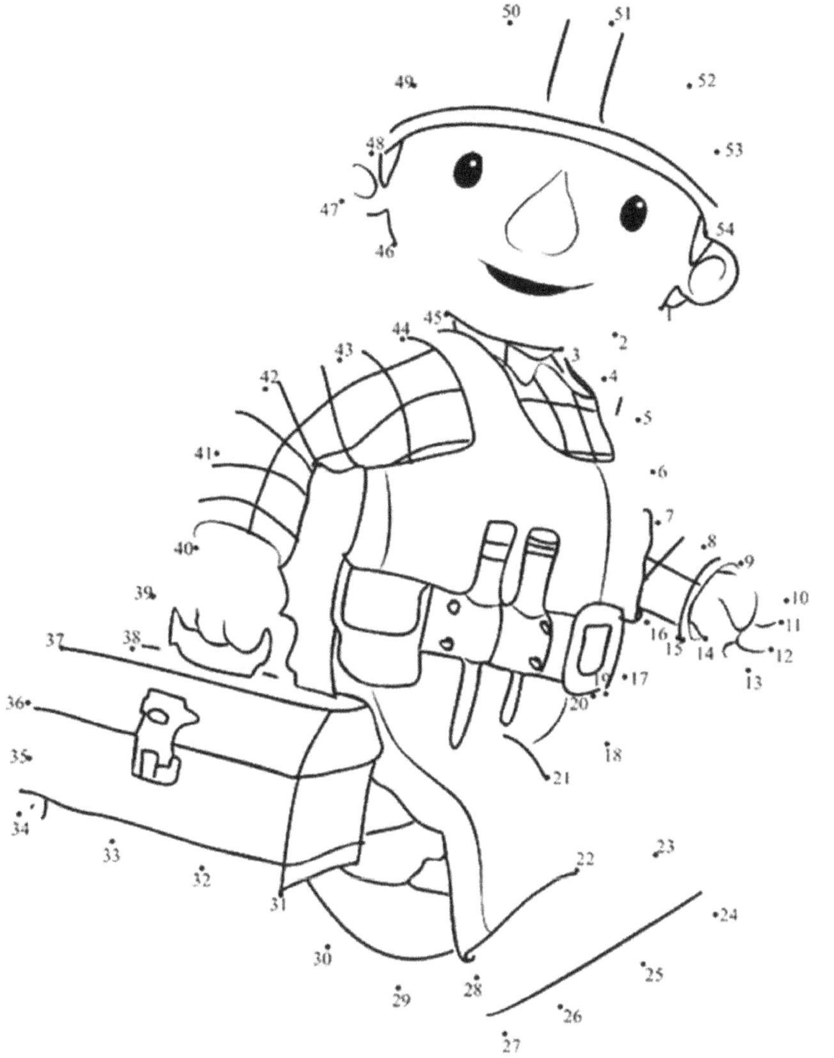

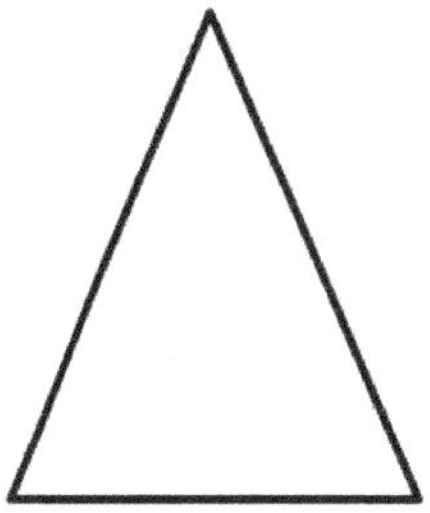

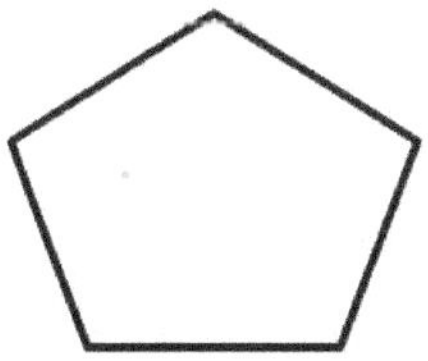

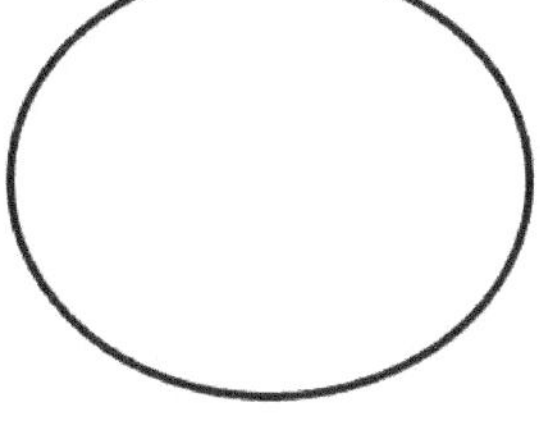

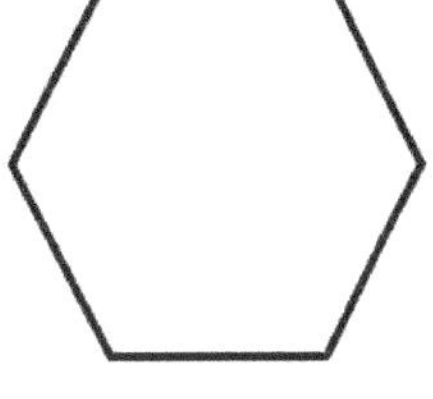

Example: Following figures show different types of triangles.

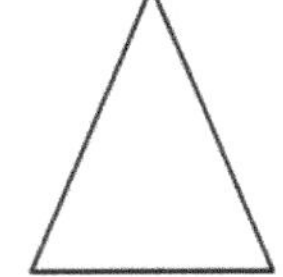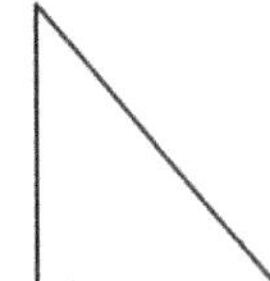

13: Find a suitable number sentence for representing the following grid pattern.

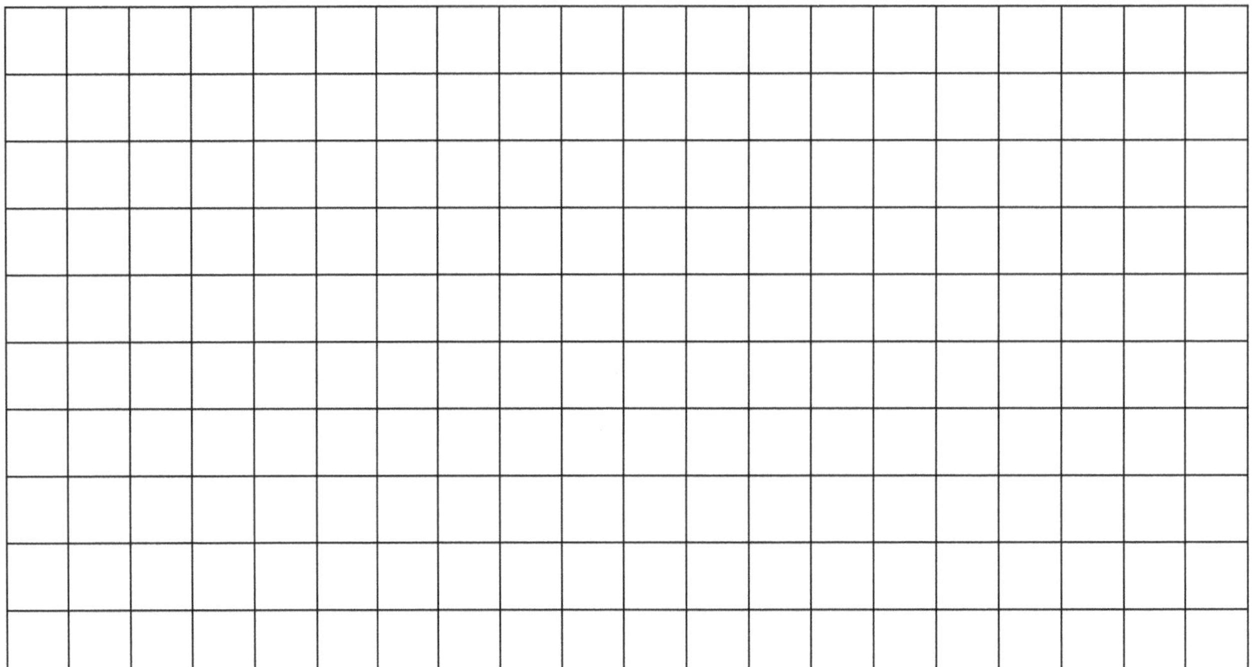

_______ X _______ = 200; 20 X ____ = 200; ____ X 10 = _______.

Aid Box:

Find the product.

14. $5 \times 1 =$ _______

15. _______ $= 10 \times 2$

16. _______ $= 4 \times 5$

17. $10 \times 10 =$ _______

18. $10 \times 0 =$ _______

19. $10 \times 5 =$ _______

20. _______ $= 1 \times 5$

21. _______ $= 5 \times 9$

22. 3
  $\times 4$

23. 5
  $\times 0$

24. 4
  $\times 8$

25. 10
  $\times 5$

26. 10
  $\times 9$

27. 10
  $\times 1$

28. 10
  $\times 8$

29. 9
  $\times 2$

30. 4
  $\times 10$

31. 5
  $\times 9$

32. 5
  $\times 0$

33. 5
  $\times 7$

34: Number Table:

Use a multiplication table.

Find the product 6 × 8 where row 6 and column 8 meet.

6 × 8 = _______

- Shade the row for 3 in the table. Then, compare the rows for 3 and 6. What do you notice about their products?

____

____

×	0	1	2	3	4	5	6	7	8	9	10
0	0	0	0	0	0	0	0	0	0	0	0
1	0	1	2	3	4	5	6	7	8	9	10
2	0	2	4	6	8	10	12	14	16	18	20
3	0	3	6	9	12	15	18	21	24	27	30
4	0	4	8	12	16	20	24	28	32	36	40
5	0	5	10	15	20	25	30	35	40	45	50
6	0	6	12	18	24	30	36	42	48	54	60
7	0	7	14	21	28	35	42	49	56	63	70
8	0	8	16	24	32	40	48	56	64	72	80
9	0	9	18	27	36	45	54	63	72	81	90
10	0	10	20	30	40	50	60	70	80	90	100

By using above mentioned number table find the following:

(8 X 9) + (4 X 7) = __________;

(6 X 9) + (4 X 4) = __________;

35: Observe the pattern and write another such attern.

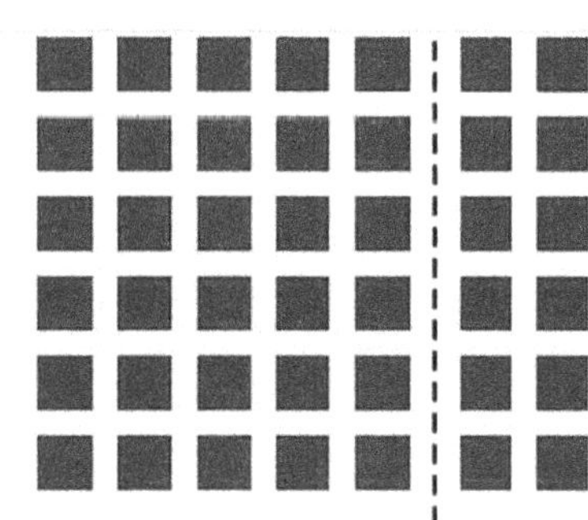

6 x 7   = 42

         = 6 X (5 + 2)

         = 6 X 5 + 6 X 2

         = 30 + 12

6 X 5 = 30   6 X 2 = 12

8 X 9 = 8 X ____ + 8 X ____ = 8 X (____ + ____)

9 X 6 = 9 X ____ + 9 X ____ = 9 X (____ + ____)

7 X 5 = 7 X ____ + 7 X ____ = 7 X (____ + ____)

36: Complete the following –

$8 \times 9 = (4 + 4) \times 9$

$8 \times 9 = (\underline{\quad} \times \underline{\quad}) + (\underline{\quad} \times \underline{\quad})$

$8 \times 9 = \underline{\quad} + \underline{\quad}$

$8 \times 9 = \underline{\quad}$

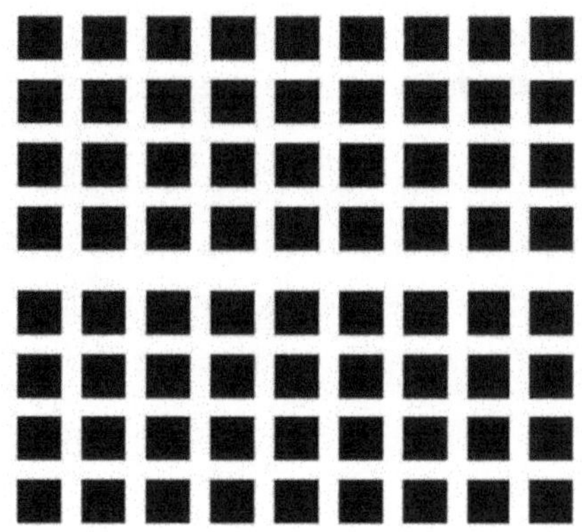

Aid Box:---

1. $2 \times \underline{\quad} = 8$ 2. $30 \div 5 = \underline{\quad}$ 3. $16 \div 2 = \underline{\quad}$

4. $45 \div 5 = \underline{\quad}$ 5. $5 \times \underline{\quad} = 25$ 6. $8 \div 2 = \underline{\quad}$

7. $5 \times \underline{\quad} = 15$ 8. $2 \times \underline{\quad} = 20$ 9. $2 \times \underline{\quad} = 12$

Find each quotient.

10. $18 \div 2 = \underline{\quad}$ 11. $35 \div 5 = \underline{\quad}$ 12. $40 \div 5 = \underline{\quad}$

13. $4 \div 2 = \underline{\quad}$ 14. $10 \div 2 = \underline{\quad}$ 15. $5 \div 5 = \underline{\quad}$

16. $5 \overline{)30}$ 17. $2 \overline{)14}$ 18. $5 \overline{)20}$ 19. $5 \overline{)5}$

20. $2 \overline{)12}$ 21. $2 \overline{)8}$ 22. $5 \overline{)15}$ 23. $5 \overline{)40}$

Complete.

24. $20 \div 2 = \underline{\quad}$ 25. $15 \div 5 = \underline{\quad} \times 1$ 26. $40 \div 5 = \underline{\quad} \times 2$

27. $9 \times 3 \times \underline{\quad} = 81$ 28. $\underline{\quad} \times 6 \times 2 = 12$ 29. $9 \times \underline{\quad} = 63$

Achiever A

I: Solve the following:

1. $36 \div 4$ 2. $21 \div 3$ 3. $28 \div 4$

_______________   _______________   _______________

_______________   _______________   _______________

Find each quotient.

4. $18 \div 3 =$ _____   5. $32 \div 4 =$ _____   6. $30 \div 3 =$ _____

7. $8 \div 2 =$ _____   8. $12 \div 3 =$ _____   9. $12 \div 4 =$ _____

10. $3\overline{)15}$ 11. $4\overline{)28}$ 12. $3\overline{)27}$ 13. $4\overline{)16}$

14. $4\overline{)32}$ 15. $3\overline{)9}$ 16. $4\overline{)8}$ 17. $3\overline{)30}$

Complete.

18. $12 \div 4 =$ _____ $\times 3$ 19. $24 \div 4 =$ _____ $\times 3$ 20. $27 \div 3 =$ _____ $\times 3$

II: Find number of lines of symmetry in each case.

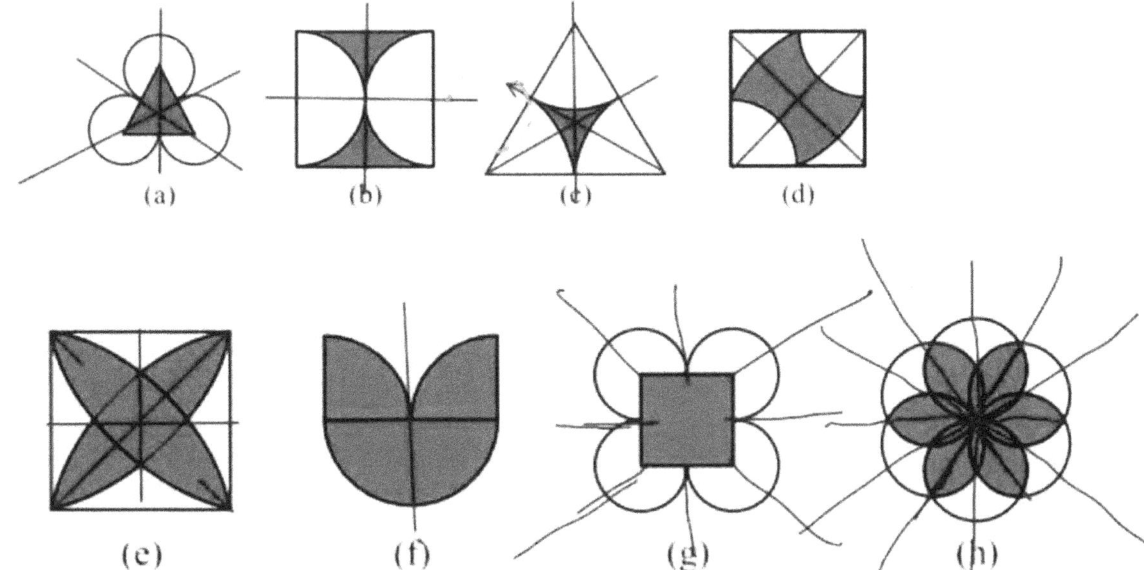

(a)   (b)   (c)   (d)

(e)   (f)   (g)   (h)

Achiever B

I: Complete the following –

1. $7 \div 7 =$ _____
2. $0 \div 5 =$ _____
3. $4 \div 1 =$ _____

4. $8 \div 1 =$ _____
5. $6 \div 6 =$ _____
6. $0 \div 3 =$ _____

7. $2 \div 2 =$ _____
8. $0 \div 8 =$ _____
9. $2 \div 1 =$ _____

10. $0 \div 4 =$ _____
11. $3 \div 1 =$ _____
12. $5 \div 5 =$ _____

13. $4 \div 4 =$ _____
14. $9 \div 1 =$ _____
15. $0 \div 2 =$ _____

16. $7 \div 1 =$ _____
17. $9 \div 9 =$ _____
18. $6 \div 1 =$ _____

19. $0 \div 1 =$ _____
20. $0 \div 9 =$ _____
21. $3 \div 3 =$ _____

Compare. Write $<$, $>$, or $=$ for each $\bigcirc$.

22. $7 \div 7 \bigcirc 7 \div 1$
23. $9 \div 9 \bigcirc 10 - 9$
24. $5 \div 1 \bigcirc 5 + 1$

25. $0 \div 6 \bigcirc 6 + 0$
26. $2 + 4 \bigcirc 0 \div 6$
27. $3 \div 1 \bigcirc 3 \times 1$

28.
$$\begin{array}{r} 475 \\ - 352 \\ \hline \end{array}$$

29.
$$\begin{array}{r} 450 \\ + 640 \\ \hline \end{array}$$

30.
$$\begin{array}{r} 7,991 \\ - 4,328 \\ \hline \end{array}$$

31.
$$\begin{array}{r} 665 \\ + 392 \\ \hline \end{array}$$

II: write a suitable number sentence for counting number of stars present in the following grid.

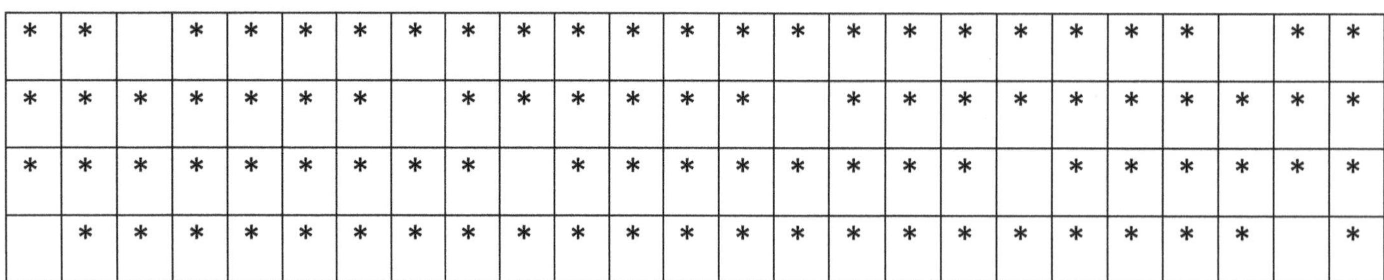

_______ X _______ - _______ = _____________ .

Achiever C

Find the missing factor or quotient.

1. 7 × ______ = 42   2. 30 ÷ 6 = ______   3. 16 ÷ 8 = ______

4. 36 ÷ 6 = ______   5. 8 × ______ = 56   6. 21 ÷ 7 = ______

7. 7 × ______ = 63   8. 6 × ______ = 48   9. 8 × ______ = 72

Find the quotient.

10. 18 ÷ 6 = ______   11. 32 ÷ 8 = ______   12. 40 ÷ 8 = ______

13. 49 ÷ 7 = ______   14. 12 ÷ 6 = ______   15. 35 ÷ 7 = ______

16. $7\overline{)14}$ 17. $7\overline{)28}$ 18. $6\overline{)24}$ 19. $7\overline{)14}$

20. $7\overline{)63}$ 21. $6\overline{)30}$ 22. $6\overline{)54}$ 23. $8\overline{)24}$

Complete.

24. 36 ÷ 6 = ______ × 3   25. 56 ÷ 7 = ______ + 3   26. 8 ÷ 8 = ______ − 3

Write the numbers in order from greatest to least.

27. 19	28. 2,013	29. 315	30. 30,500
43	2,130	272	30,099
38	3,120	156	30,122

______   ______   ______   ______

______   ______   ______   ______

31 : Arrange the following in ascending order:

21 tousands, 121 hundreds,   121,121;   12 hundreds and 12;   210,109;

32: (19 + 19 + ... 100 times) + (81 + 81 + ... 100 times) = ______________.

Achiever D

Complete the following:

1. $9 \times$ _____ $= 45$ 2. $30 \div 10 =$ _____   3. $18 \div 9 =$ _____

4. $36 \div 9 =$ _____   5. $9 \times$ _____ $= 54$ 6. $20 \div 10 =$ _____

7. $9 \times$ _____ $= 81$ 8. $10 \times$ _____ $= 80$ 9. $10 \times$ _____ $= 40$

Find the quotient.

10. $72 \div 9 =$ _____   11. $63 \div 9 =$ _____   12. $40 \div 8 =$ _____

13. $60 \div 10 =$ _____   14. $9 \div 1 =$ _____   15. $81 \div 9 =$ _____

16. $10\overline{)10}$ 17. $9\overline{)27}$ 18. $9\overline{)54}$ 19. $10\overline{)70}$

20. $9\overline{)63}$ 21. $9\overline{)90}$ 22. $10\overline{)90}$ 23. $10\overline{)100}$

Complete.

24. $54 \div 9 =$ _____ $\times 3$ 25. $80 \div 10 =$ _____ $- 7$ 26. $36 \div 9 =$ _____ $+ 3$

Write $+$, $-$, $\times$, or $\div$ for each $\bigcirc$.

27. $36 \bigcirc 4 = 9$ 28. $18 \bigcirc 6 = 12$

29. $9 \bigcirc 3 = 27$ 30. $16 \bigcirc 8 = 24$

Solve.

31. Divide 45 by 5.   32. Divide 24 by 6.   33. Divide 48 by 8.

_____________   _____________   _____________

Write the time.

34. 18 minutes   35. 18 minutes   36. 20 minutes
    after noon   before noon   before 1:15 P.M.

37. $(9 + 9 + 9$ ...... 1,000 times $) + (10 + 10 + ...$ 100 times $) =$ ___________.

Achiever E

Write a division sentence for each.

1. 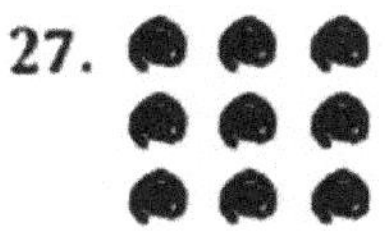

2. 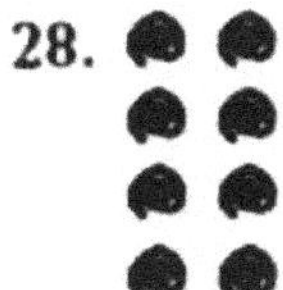

3.

$$\begin{array}{cc} 20 & 10 \\ -10 & -10 \\ \hline 10 & 0 \end{array}$$

_______________   _______________   _______________

Find the missing factor or quotient.

4. $50 \div 5 =$ _______

5. $7 \times$ _______ $= 49$

6. $45 \div 9 =$ _______

7. $6 \times$ _______ $= 54$

8. $72 \div 8 =$ _______

9. $4 \times$ _______ $= 40$

Find the quotient.

10. $36 \div 6 =$ _______

11. $24 \div 8 =$ _______

12. $42 \div 7 =$ _______

13. $56 \div 8 =$ _______

14. $63 \div 7 =$ _______

15. $14 \div 2 =$ _______

16. $8\overline{)64}$

17. $10\overline{)10}$

18. $5\overline{)35}$

19. $9\overline{)27}$

20. $7\overline{)70}$

21. $5\overline{)30}$

22. $4\overline{)36}$

23. $7\overline{)49}$

Compare. Write $<$, $>$, or $=$ for each $\bigcirc$.

24. $36 - 6 \bigcirc 8 \times 3$

25. $18 \div 9 \bigcirc 0 + 3$

26. $64 \div 8 \bigcirc 2 \times 4$

Write a multiplication sentence for each.

27. 

28. 29. 30. 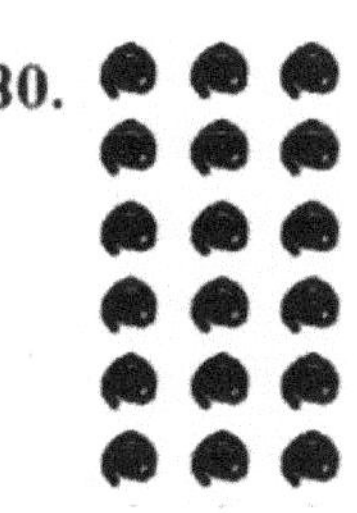

31: 15 times 100 + 85 times 100 = _________ times 100 = ______ X 100 = _________.

32: Smallest odd number of four digits which also divisible by 3 = ___________.

Achiever F

Complete the following:

1. $9 \times 1 = $ _________

$9 \times 10 = $ _________

$9 \times 100 = $ _________

$9 \times 1,000 = $ _________

3. $7 \times 4 = $ _________

_________ $\times 40 = 280$

$7 \times$ _________ $= 2,800$

$7 \times 4,000 = $ _________

2. $6 \times 3 = $ _________

$6 \times 30 = $ _________

$6 \times 300 = $ _________

$6 \times 3,000 = $ _________

4. $6 \times 5 = $ _________

_________ $\times 50 = 300$

$6 \times$ _________ $= 3,000$

$6 \times 5,000 = $ _________

Use mental math and basic facts to complete.

5. $7 \times 80 = $ ______

6. $9 \times$ ______ $= 45,000$

7. ______ $\times 60 = 240$

8. $2 \times$ ______ $= 1,400$

9. $7 \times$ ______ $= 42,000$

10. ______ $\times 800 = 2,400$

11. ______ $\times 20 = 180$

12. $5 \times 500 = $ ______

13. $5 \times 4,000 = $ ______

14. $3 \times$ ______ $= 210$

15. $1 \times$ ______ $= 1,000$

16. $5 \times 200 = $ ______

Find the product or quotient.

17.	18.	19.	20.	21.
35	62	58	47	24
$\times 7$	$\times 7$	$\times 3$	$\times 5$	$\times 6$

22. $36 \div 6 = $ _________

23. $18 \div 6 = $ _________

24. $10 \times 6 = $ _________

25. $10 \times 91 + 10 \times 9 = 10 \times ($ ____ $+$ ____ $) = 10 \times$ ______ $= $ _________.

26. How many times $10 = 10,000$?

Achiever G

Complete the following:

1. $36 \div 4 =$ _____

    $360 \div 4 =$ _____

    $3{,}600 \div 4 =$ _____

2. $54 \div 6 =$ _____

    $540 \div 6 =$ _____

    $5{,}400 \div 6 =$ _____

3. $25 \div 5 =$ _____

    _____ $\div 5 = 50$

    $2{,}500 \div 5 =$ _____

4. $27 \div 9 =$ _____

    _____ $\div 9 = 30$

    $2{,}700 \div$ _____ $= 300$

5. $18 \div 2 =$ _____

    _____ $\div 2 = 90$

    $1{,}800 \div$ _____ $= 900$

6. $49 \div 7 =$ _____

    $490 \div 7 =$ _____

    _____ $\div 7 = 700$

Use mental math and a basic fact to find the quotient.

7. $2{,}000 \div 5 =$ _____

8. $5{,}600 \div 7 =$ _____

9. $3{,}000 \div 6 =$ _____

10. $900 \div 3 =$ _____

11. $1{,}500 \div 5 =$ _____

12. $2{,}800 \div 4 =$ _____

13. $450 \div 9 =$ _____

14. $6{,}300 \div 7 =$ _____

15. $640 \div 8 =$ _____

16. $400 \div 5 =$ _____

17. $3{,}500 \div 7 =$ _____

18. $200 \div 2 =$ _____

19. $1{,}600 \div 4 =$ _____

20. $6{,}000 \div 2 =$ _____

21. $250 \div 5 =$ _____

Find the quotient.

22. $8\overline{)36}$

23. $9\overline{)46}$

24. $8\overline{)76}$

25. $7\overline{)43}$

Find the product.

26. $8 \times 6 =$ _____

27. $7 \times 9 =$ _____

28. $4 \times 7 =$ _____

29. $6 \times 6 =$ _____

30. $10 \times 5 =$ _____

31. $8 \times 3 =$ _____

32. $5 \times 7 =$ _____

33. $9 \times 8 =$ _____

34. $7 \times 8 =$ _____

Achiever H

Measurements:

1. the length of a table

2. the length of a pine cone

____

____

3. the length of a driveway

4. the distance to a neighboring town

____

____

Choose the best unit of measure. Write _inches, feet, yards,_ or _miles._

5. A pencil is about

5 __________ long.

6. The distance from your home to the library is about 2

__________.

7. A bike is about

4 __________ long.

8. The football player kicked

the ball 45 __________.

9. Peter grew almost

2 __________ in one year.

10. A man is about

6 __________ tall.

Find each product.

11. $7 \times 2 =$ ______

12. ______ $= 9 \times 5$

13. $6 \times 6 =$ ______

Find each quotient.

14. $14 \div 2 =$ ______

15. $27 \div 3 =$ ______

16. ______ $= 18 \div 6$

17. $24 \div 6 =$ ______

18. ______ $= 20 \div 4$

19. $8 \div 4 =$ ______

20. A ribbon measures 100 m long rope perfectly. Richimon used that ribbon 20 times to measure the rope. Maximum possible length of the tape is ______ m.

Achiever I

Complete this table.

1.

Meters	1	2	3							
Centimeters	100	200								

For 2–3, use the completed table above.

2. Gary needs 500 centimeters of space for a bookcase. How many meters of space does he need?

____

3. Kara needs 9 meters of string. How many centimeters of string does she need?

____

Jake drew a line that was 3 decimeters long. How many centimeters long was his line?

4. Which table helps solve the problem? ___________

A

Kilometers	1	2	3
Meters	1,000	2,000	3,000

C

Centimeters	100	200	300
Meters	1	2	3

B

Meters	1	2	3
Decimeters	10	20	30

D

Decimeters	1	2	3
Centimeters	10	20	30

5. What is the solution to the problem? ___________

Draw the next 3 shapes in the pattern.

6. ▽ □ △ □ ▽ □ △ □ ▽ □ △ □ ___________

7. ○ ○ □ ○ ○ ○ □ ○ ○ ○ □ ___________

8. (21 + 21 + 21 … 1,000 times) + (79 + 79 + …. 1,000 times) = ___________ .

Achiever J

1. Rani is buying light bulbs for her Christmas decorations. She buys 1020 but when she gets to the cash, she has to put back 3 hundred 13 because they are broken. How many light bulbs does Marie buy?

2. There are two combinations of packs containing Cakes and Biscuits. Packet one containing 6 cakes and 5 biscuitsls costs Rs 128. Packet B containing 5 cakes and 6 biscuits costs Rs 103. Calculate the cost of a new pack containing 10 cakes and 10 biscuits of such type?

   A: Rs. 250   B: Rs. 120

   C: Rs. 135   D: Rs. 210

3. Last Thursday in the calendar it was 27th February 2020. The forthcoming Thursday will be __________March 2020.

   A: 4   B: 5   C: 6   D: 7

4. The product of 10th multiple of 11 and the 7th multiple of 109 has __________ at its one's place.

   A: 0   B: 1   C: 2   D: 3

5. If 36 X 121 = 4,356 , then :

   a) 36X10 X 100 =

   b) 36X 400 =

   c) 36 X 200 =

   d) 36 X 1,000 =

6. $121{,}121 \div 121 =$

   A: 11   B: 101

   C: 110   D:1001

7. Some of the statements regarding prime and composite numbers are given below.

   I : 1 is not a prime *or* composite number.

   II : Two is the only even prime number.

   III: All odd numbers are not prime.

   IV: All composite numbers can be written as product of prime numbers.

   V: 101 has only two factors 1 and the number itself. That is why it is a prime number

   Which of the above statements are true?

   A: Only I   B: All

   C: I, II and III   D: Only II, III and IV

8. Product of all the factors of 6 = ___________
   A: 36   B: 12
   C: 18   D: 24

9. 121, 165 and 594 have following things in common:

   I. All these numbers are multiples of 11.

   II. These are square numbers and also are in a   pattern of incremental type. .

   III. Prime factors of these numbers are different.

Select which of the statements mentioned above are true.

A: Only I

B: Only II

C: Both I and III

D: All I, II and III

10. If we continue the following pattern:

2,000 1,750 1,500 1,250 , a , b , c

and a X b X c = d; then the digits at ones, tens and hundreds place of d respectively are

A: 1,2,3   B: 2,1,3

C: 0, 0,0   D: 1, 1, 1

11. Observe the following numbers represented in expanded form.

30,550   = 50 + a + 500

809,100 = 800,000 + 100 + _b

725,608 = 20,000 + 700,000 + 8 + c + 5,000

I.   Numbers are represented in the International System.

II.   All a, b and c are in thousands.

III.   Sum total of a, b and c exceeds 60,000.

IV.   In ascending order c > b > a.

V.   Which of the statements are true?

A: I, II and IV   B: Only IV   C: None

12. Half a dozen banana is ___a___ less than a score of it. Here a = _______

A: 20   B: 14   C: 16   D: 20

13.. Observe factors of 12 and 36 ….

Factors of 36 are   1,36,2,18,3,**12,6**,9,4

Factors of   12 are 1,**12**, 2, **6** , 3, **4**,

If common factors of 12 and 36 arranged from least to greatest are   a, b, c,

and if a x b + c = d, then d = _____

A: 24   B: 36

C: 72   D: 48

14. Height of a tree is 2 m more than a building but 3 m less than a telephone

tower. If telephone tower is 50 m tall, then find the sum total of heights of all

the three objects.

A: 212 m   B: 125 m

C: 142 m   D: 165 m

15. There are _____ diagonals in a rhombus.

16. Observe the following:

12,345 = P + 2,000 + 300 + 40 + 5;

29,658 = 20,000 + Q + R   + 50 + 8;

P is _____________ more than Q + R;

A: 4   B: 40   C: 400   D: 4000

17. 3 less than 6,000 is added to a five digit greatest number. The sum total is

then rounded up to nearest thousands. Find the value.

A: 16,000   B: 60,000   C: 10,600   D: 16,200

18. 5th multiple of 600 and 6th multiple of 500 multiplied to obtain a value which is

_____________ less than the smallest 6 digit number.

A: 30,000   B: 50,000   C: 40,000   D: 66,000

19. 100th multiple of the product of all the factors of 8 is _______ more than the

6th multiple of 1,000.

A: 200   B: 400

C: 500   D: 600

20. There are ____ faces , _____ edges and _____ vertices in a hexagonal Prism.

21. Temperature of a city increased by $5\,^{0}$ C last week. If a corresponding increase

of temperature in ^{0} F is 1.8 times more than that of the value in ^{0} C , then find

the value of such increase of temperature in ^{0} F

A: 18^{0} F   B: 9^{0} F   C: 8.9^{0} F   D: $6\,^{0}$ F

22. Half of a quarter of four digit smallest number exceeds the greatest two digit

number by P. If we multiply P by half of it then the value represents a _____

multiple of 13.

A: 24   B: 25

C: 26   D: 27

23. There are ____ more edges and ____ more vertices in a cuboid than in a

rectangular pyramid.

24. (11 + 11 + 11 + ……. 2,000 times) = _____ X 1,000

Achiever K

1. Write a number greater than 1, 50, 000 by using digits 5, 4 and 2.

2. 324 thousands = _____________________ tens.

3. 32 crore = _____________ thousands.

4. _____________ crore is 400 greater than 99,99,600.

5. Write a number smaller than 39 lakhs by using digits 4, 3 and 8. Digits can be repeated.

6. Write the predecessor of 7 digit greatest number.

7. Calculate the sum total of place values of 3 in the following numbers

8.   34,55,67,505,   30,56,05,506 and 35,05,04,050

9. Difference of the place value and face value of 8 in 65,76,80,653, 78,806 and 48,65,678 = _______________.

10. _____,00,00,000 = 18 crore.

11. Numbers divisible by 2 are also called _____________ numbers.

12. _____ is the only even prime number.

13. All prime numbers have only _______ factors. _____ and the number itself.

14. Sum total of 2 eve numbers is always an _________ number.

15. Sum total of an even number and an odd number is always an _______ number.

16. A prime number between 95 and 100 = _____________.

17. All the multiples of 8 are also multiples of 2 and _______.

18. All the multiples of _____ and 4 may or may not be a multiple of 8.

19. All the multiples of ___ and ____ are not necessarily multiples of 10.

20. All multiples of 10 are also multiples of _____ and _____.

Aid Box ---

1. <1 = <2 = <COD. Find the supplementary angle of <1.
a)   Identify two pairs of adjacent angles.
b)   Reflex angle of <2 = ____.
c)   <AOD = ________.
d)   Reflex angle of <AOD = __.
e)   Supplement of <2 = _____.

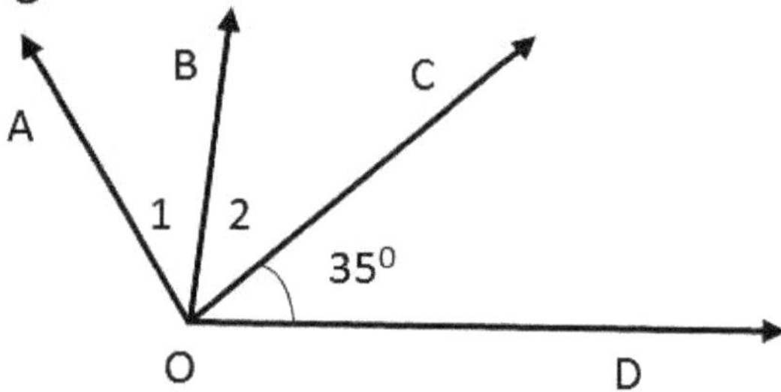

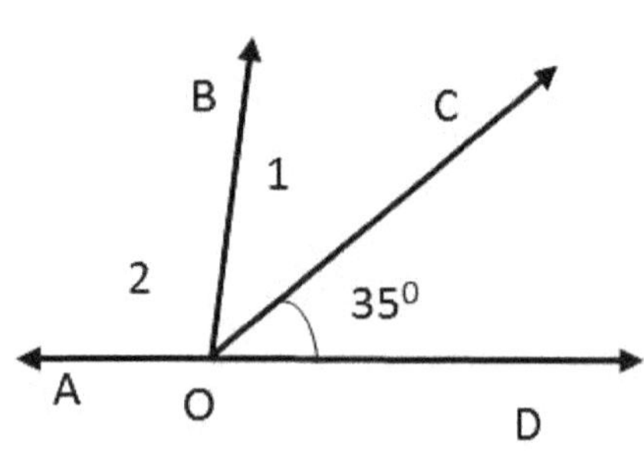

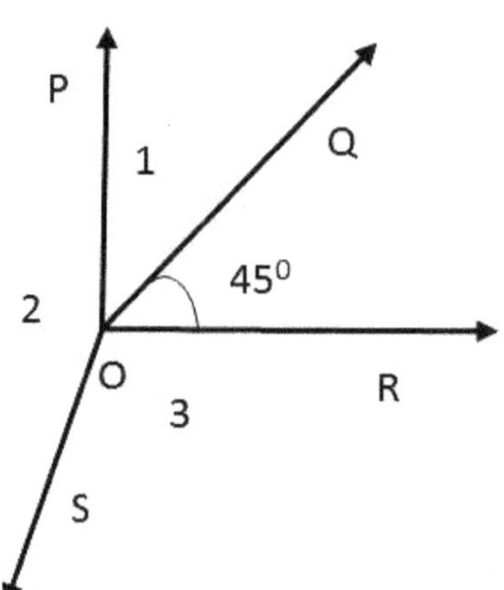

2. OC bisects <BOD.
<1 = _______;
<2 = _______;
Identify 2 sets of linear pairs.

3. <1 = 2/3rd of <QOR
   <2 = 5 times <1;
   Find all the angles.

Achiever L

1: Write at least three facts through wich following group of numbers are related.

A: 21, 7,3   B: 8, 11, 88   C: 4, 9, 36   D: 36, 9 , 4

2: how many even numbers are there in between a and 51?

3. Observe the Prime number chart and answer the following

2	3	5	7	11	13	17	19	23	
29	31	37	41	43	47	53	59	61	67
71	73	79	83	89	97	101	103	107	109
113	127	131	137	139	149	151	157	163	167
173	179	181	191	193	197	199			

    a.   There are ______ prime numbers in between 1 and 200.

    b.   There are ________ Prime numbers greater than 150 and less than 200.

    c.   _____ and ______ are a pair of consecutive prime number.

    d.   Sum total of all the prime numbers present in the first column = ______.

4: One apple = 100, one banana = 10, one mango = 1;

21 apples + 32 bananas + 38 mangoes = ________________.

Achiever M

1. Half of a number exceeds three digit smallest number by 9. Find the number.

Find the perimeter of each figure.

2. 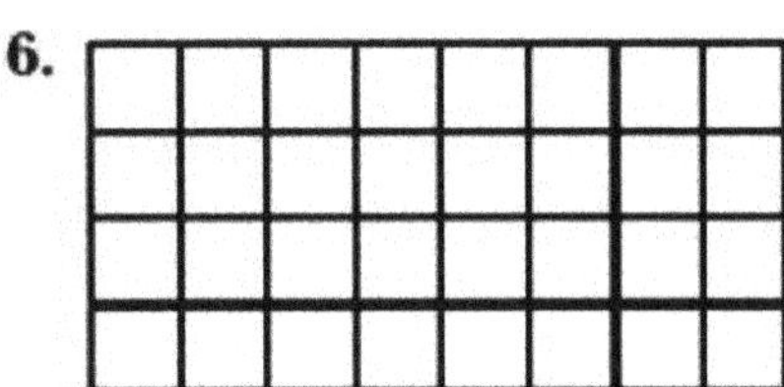

____

3. 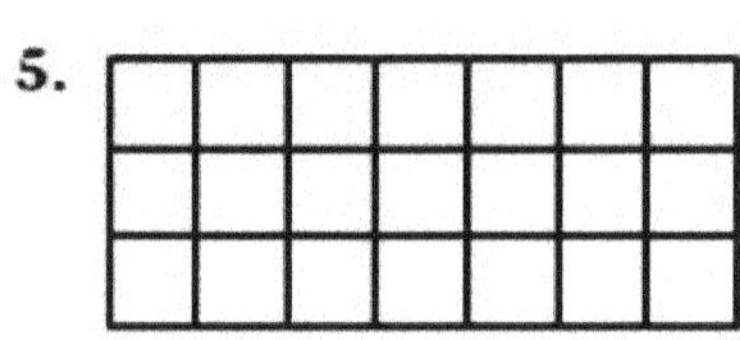

____

4.

____

5. 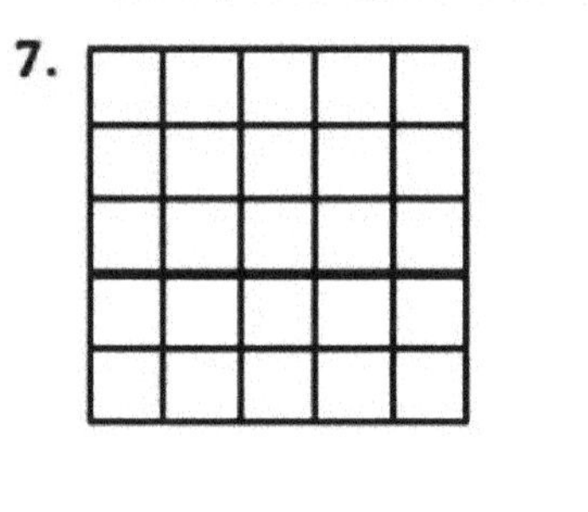

____

6.

____

7.

____

8.   716
   − 304

9.   241
   + 93

10.   876
   − 759

11. 8)56

12. 9)72

13. 8)64

12. (125 X 10,000) + (875 X 10,000) = _________ X 10,000 = __________________.

13. (500 − 5 − 5 − 5 .... 100 times) = _______________.

14. A frog jumps 50 cm during 1 jump. It has to come out of a well of depth 325 m. how many times do the frog jump?

Achiever N

1: Observe the pattern and complete it:

11 X 11   = 121;

111 X 111   = 12321;

1111 X 1111   = ____________;

______X______   = 123454321;

2: We have 4 X 25 = 100, 5 X 20 = 100 and 10 X 10 = 100 ;

    4 X 10 X 25 X 10 X 5 X 20 X 130,921 = 130,921 X ________________.

3: We consider volume of a unit cube equal to 1 cubic cm. Now find volume of the following combination of solid shapes.

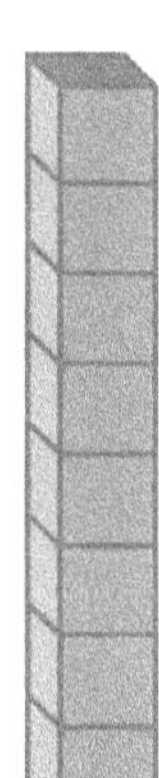  = 1 cubic cm

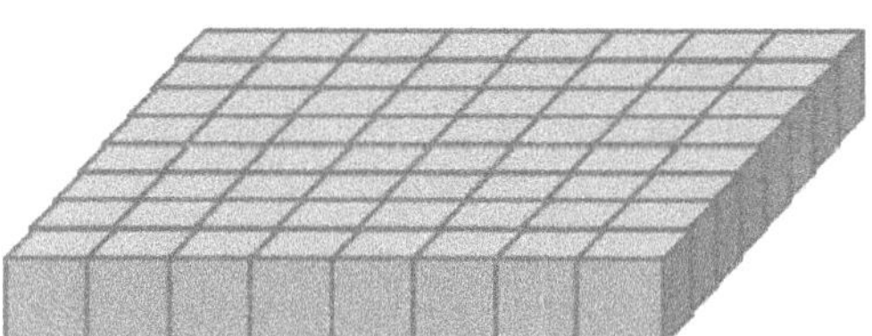 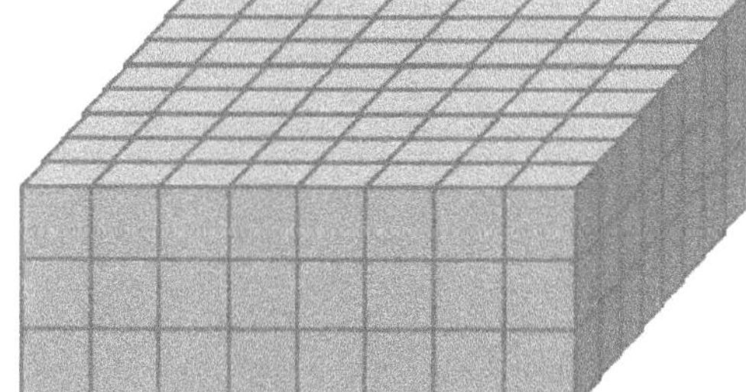

4: Find a suitable number sentence to count the number of stars present in the following grid.

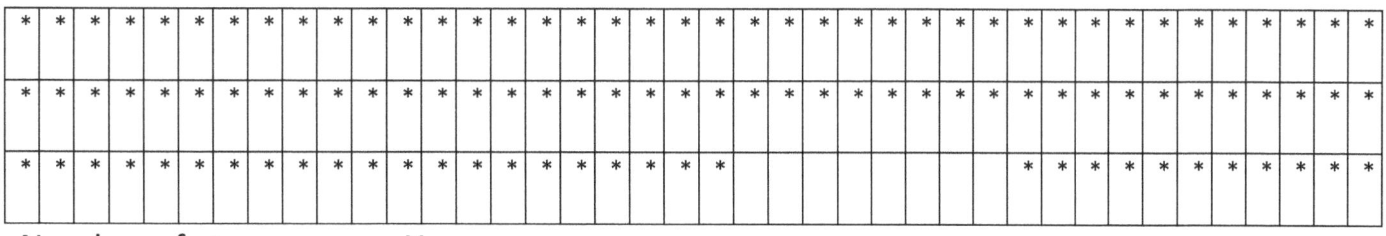

Number of stars = ______ X ________ - ________ = ________________.

5. Draw lines of symmetry and answer questions as follows.

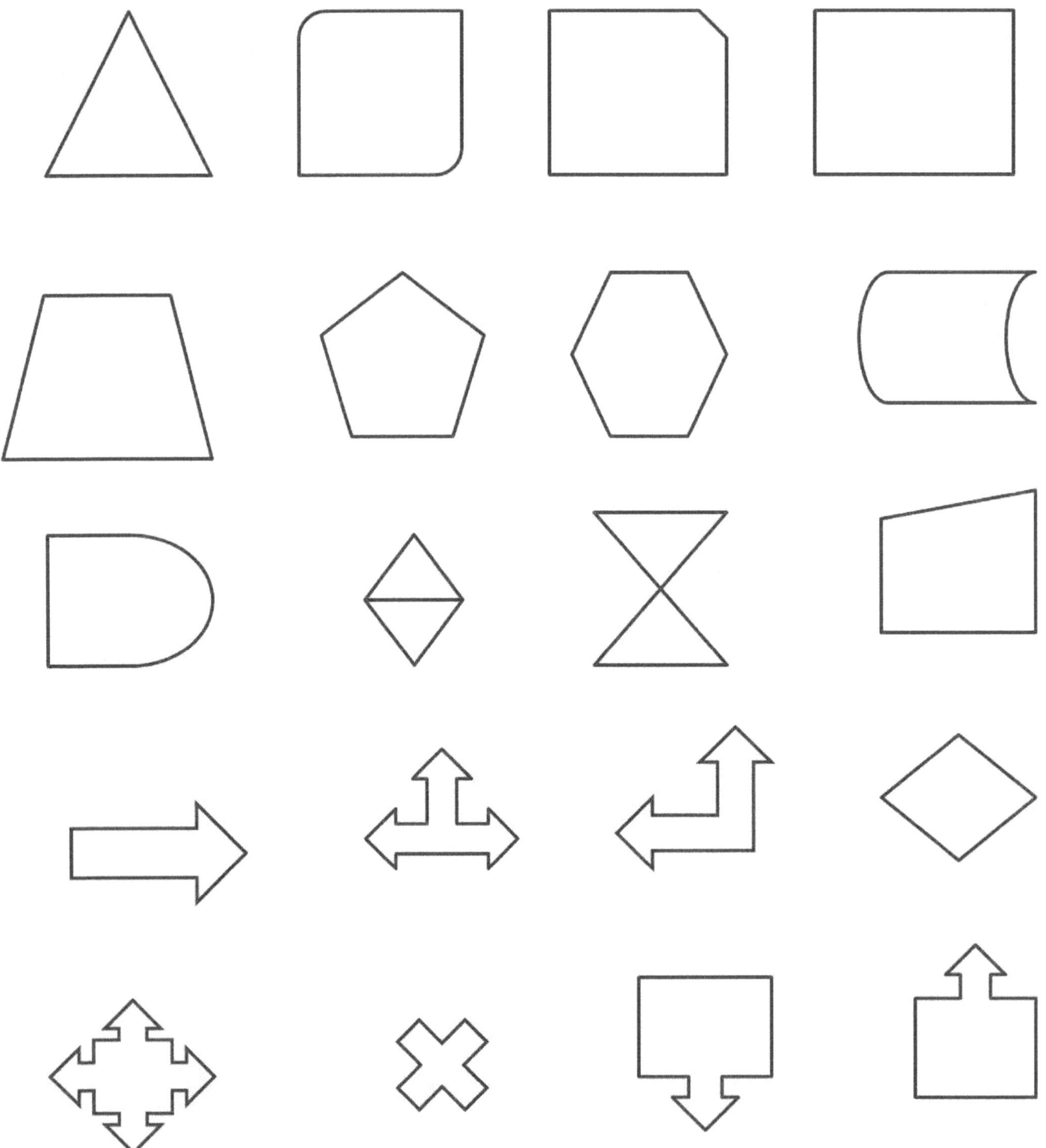

How many figures are there having no lines of symmetry?

How many figures are there having more than one lines of symmetry?

Achiever O

Find area of the following figures.

1. 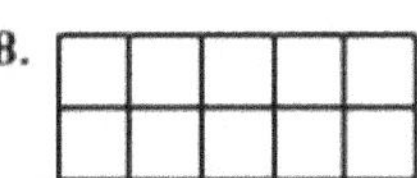

2.

3.

____________________   ____________________   ____________________

4. 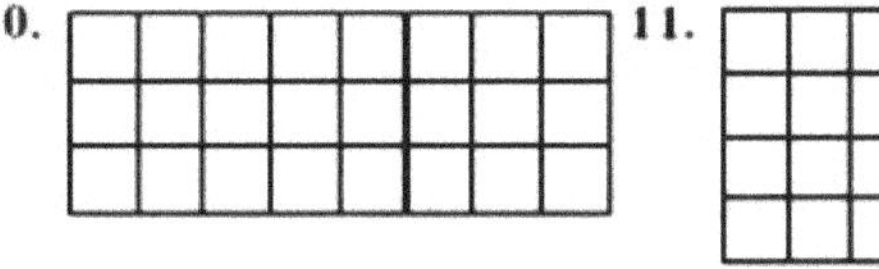

5.

6. 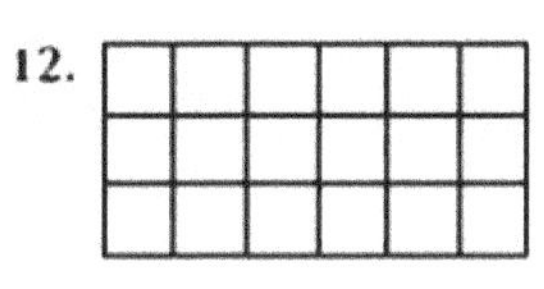

____________________   ____________________   ____________________

7.

8.

9.

____________________   ____________________   ____________________

10.

11.

12.

____________________   ____________________   ____________________

Find each missing number.

13. $4 + \_\_\_\_ = 11$

14. $5 + \_\_\_\_ = 8$

15. $9 + \_\_\_\_ = 17$

16. $2 + \_\_\_\_ = 10$

17. $\_\_\_\_ \times 8 = 64$

18. $\_\_\_\_ \times 12 = 48$

19: Moonalisha arranged 400 square sized scrap cards of side 2 cm each in two different possible ways to obtain maximum possible and minium ossible outer boundary of the figures. Find the respective perimeter of both the figures that she obtained by using square sized scrap cards.

20. $(36 + 36 + 36 + \ldots 100 \text{ times}) = 36 \times \_\_\_\_\_\_ = \_\_\_\_\_\_\_\_\_\_\_\_\_\_\_.$

Achiever P

I: Write suitable value of fraction for the following.

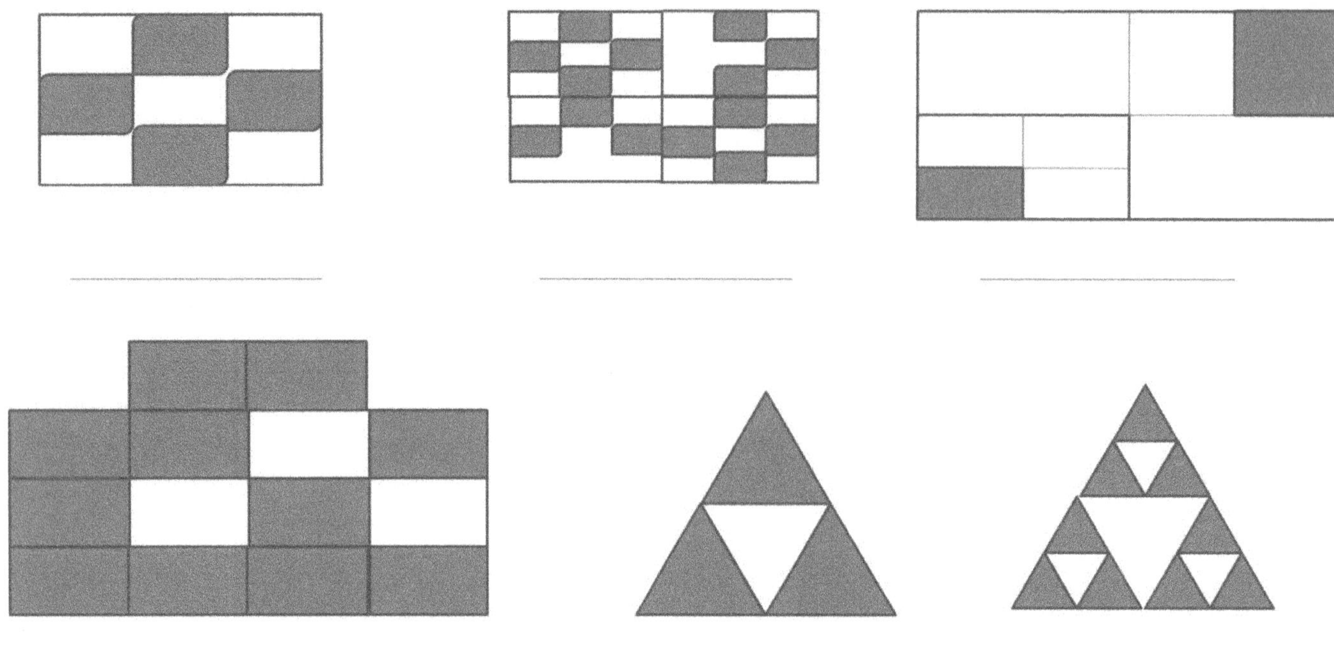

II: Provide suitable number sentence for the following.

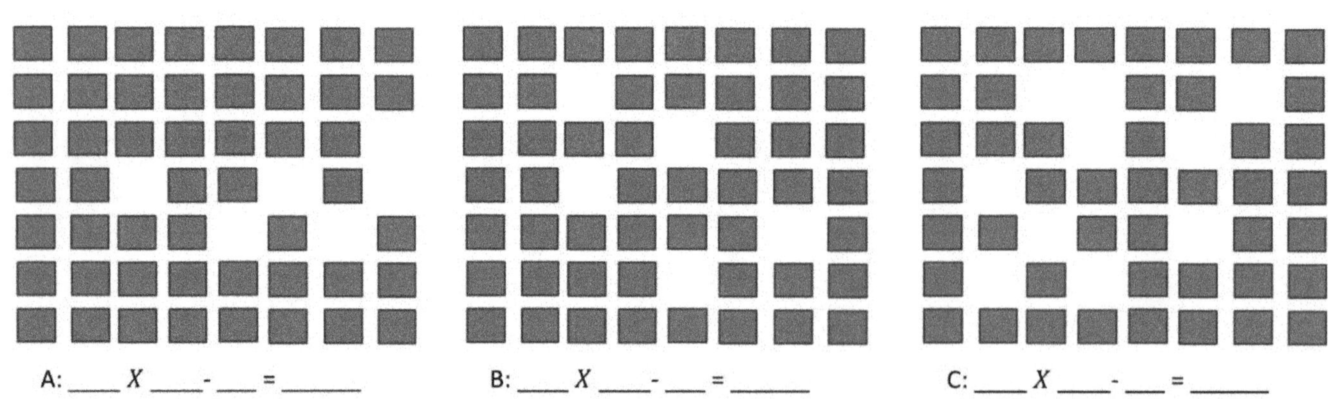

A: ____ X ____ - ___ = ______   B: ____ X ____ - ___ = ______   C: ____ X ____ - ___ = ______

III: Pandemonia collected few cards and arranged in the pattern of grid having 10 columns and 25 rows. After arranging all cards in the grid her friend Salientia lifted 15 cards from the grid. Find the card left in the grid. Also prvide suitable number sentence for your problem solving.

Achiever Q

I: Find how many figures in the following collection are not polygons.

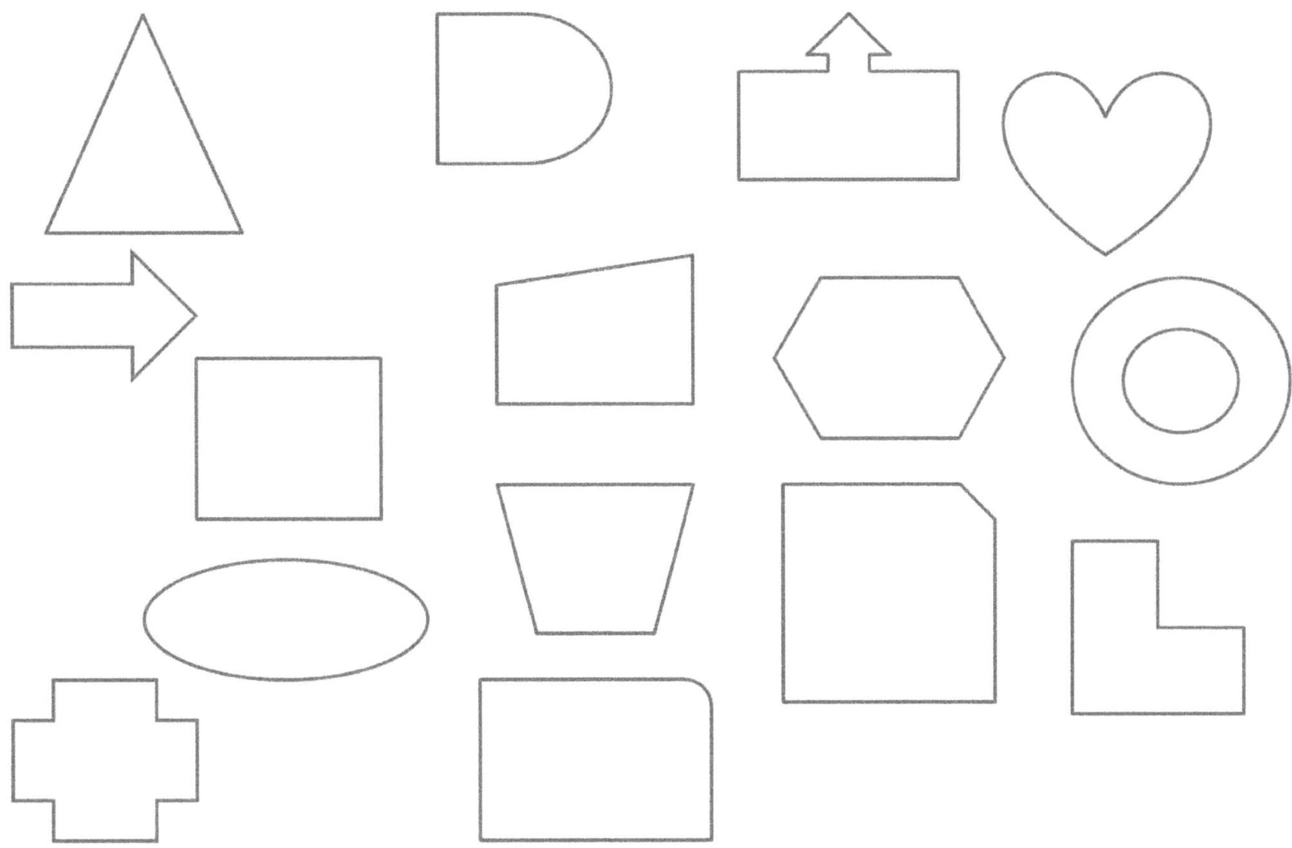

II: Draw hands of the following clocks

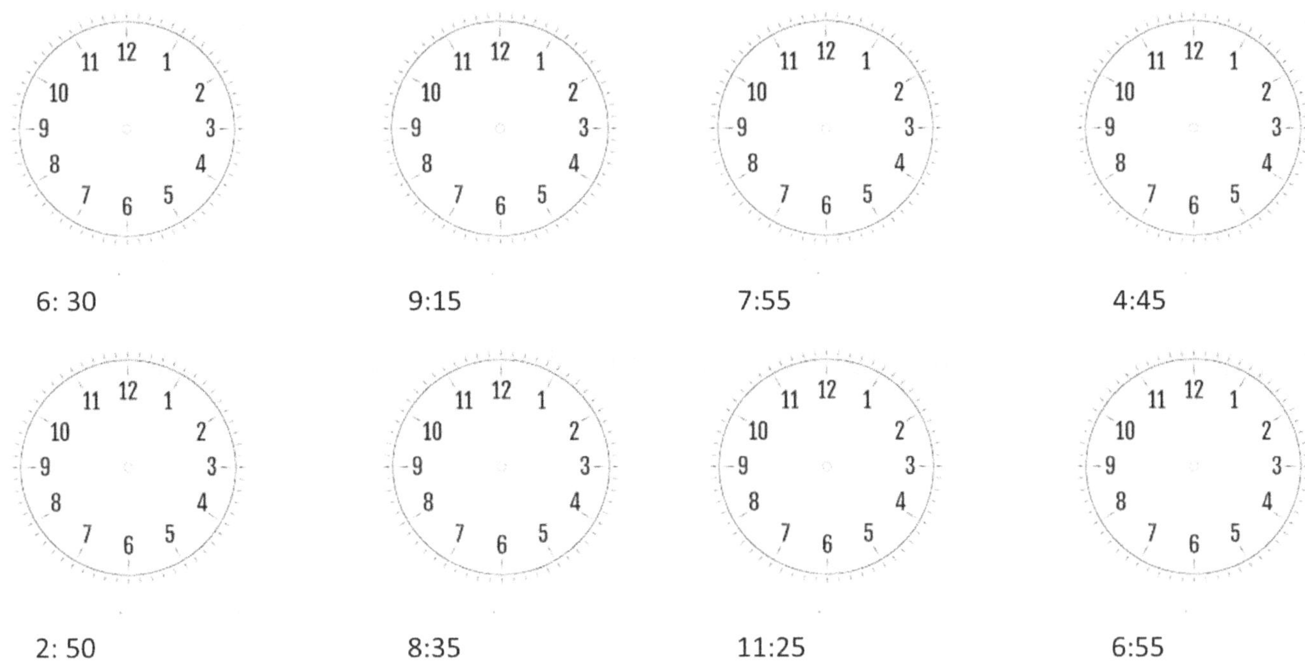

6: 30

9:15

7:55

4:45

2: 50

8:35

11:25

6:55

III. Cmlete the following task.

Writing numbers

Words	Number
Seventy seven	
Ninety five	
Sixty one	
Eighty nine	
Six hundred & sixty	
Two hundred & twenty	

Patterns

1. 2, 4, 6, ___
2. 10, 20, 30, ___
3. 12, 14, 16, ___
4. 20, 40, 60, ___
5. 13, 15, 17, ___
6. 33, 36, 39, ___

Addition

1. 14 + 7 = ___
2. 35 + 8 = ___
3. 22 + 8 = ___
4. 10 + 20 = ___
5. 17 + 9 = ___
6. 35 + 10 = ___
7. 20 + 20 = ___
8. 40 + 30 = ___
9. 60 + 10 = ___
10. 40 + 40 = ___
11. 20 + 30 = ___
12. 70 + 10 = ___

Shade even numbers

22	39	28	17	19	20	88
42	110	150	15	73	49	92
100	99	47	52	36	68	72
37	71	18	68	98	21	14

How many tens and ones?

1. 65 - Tens = ___ Ones = ___
2. 49 - Tens = ___ Ones = ___
3. 18 - Tens = ___ Ones = ___
4. 77 - Tens = ___ Ones = ___
5. 63 - Tens = ___ Ones = ___

IV: Timletomia collected sticker of birds for her scrap book. Write a suitable number sentence for counting the number of birds in her collection.

V: Jimbalgo jumps 75 cm high during one effort. How many effrots are needed to climb up from a dig of 7 m depth?

Achiever R

I: Complete the number pyramids of addition and subtraction.

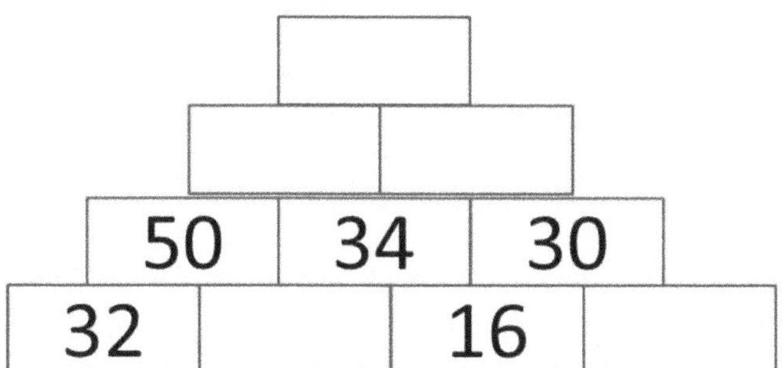

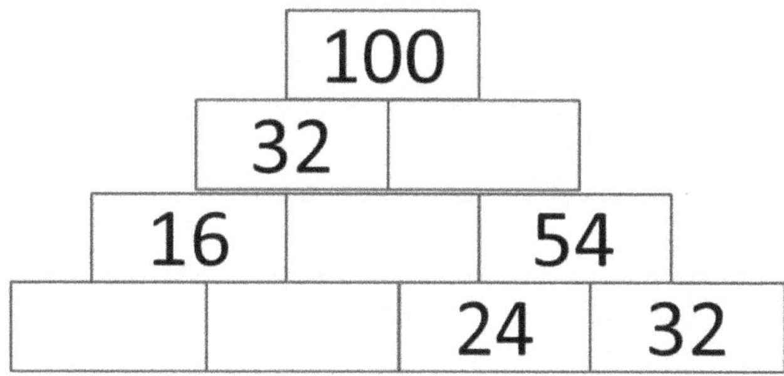

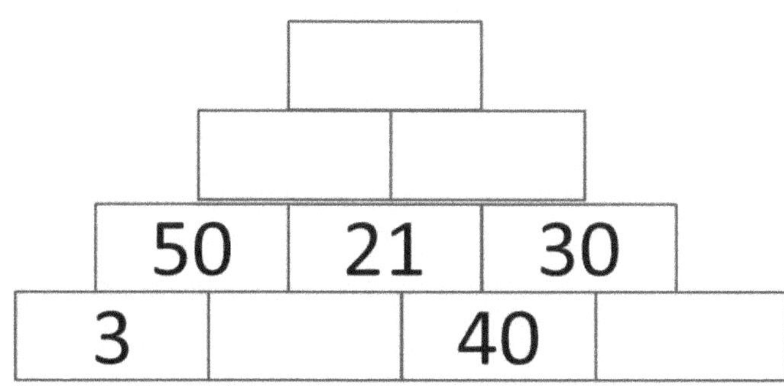

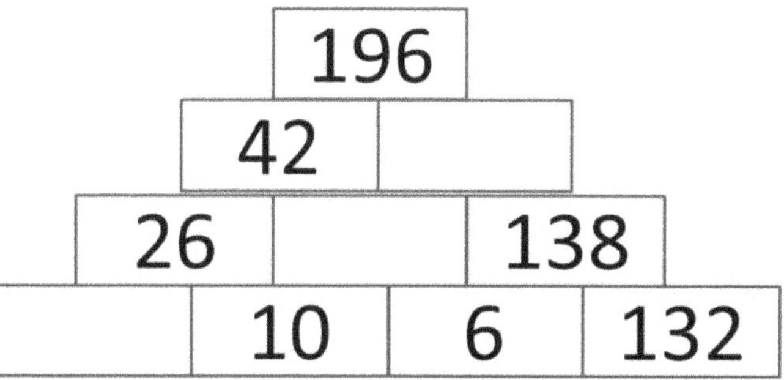

II: Complete the following pattern.

1 + 3	= 2 X 2	= 4;
1 + 3 + ____	= 3 X 3	= ___;
__ + __ + ___ + ___	= 4 X 4	= ___;
__ + __ + ___ + ___ + ___	= ____ X ____	= 25;

III: Antonio alone can paint a wall in 6 hours. He will take ____ days for painting 6 such walls while working 4 hours a day.

IV: Free time.

Across
3. 4x12
5. 50 divided by 2
8. 28 divided by 7
9. 25 divided by 5
10. 144 x12

Down
1. 7x6
2. 9x9
4. 20 x 5
6. 8x5
7. 60 divided by 12

[Hints 4 X 12 = 48; Across 3 = FORTYEIGHT]

V. Add:

1.	2.	3.
442 97,745 495,155 + 932,047	42 77 9,905 + 78,675	20 18 650,958 + 203,416

4.	5.	6.
611 52,718 5,638 + 381	7,871 129,136 4,306 + 851,640	47 65,361 20 + 26

7.	8.	9.
75 358 372 + 673,148	6,369 45,245 42,091 + 685	731,970 788 62 + 764

VI: Trace the ways out …

VII: Complete the following.

1 a. ________ × 10 = 30000	1 b. ________ × 100 = 40000
2 a. ________ × 3000 = 24000000	2 b. ________ × 600 = 12000
3 a. ________ × 300 = 150000	3 b. ________ × 90 = 9000
4 a. 700 × ________ = 63000	4 b. 5000 × ________ = 150000
5 a. 1000 × ________ = 4000000	5 b. 50 × ________ = 1000
6 a. 500 × ________ = 35000	6 b. 40 × ________ = 240000
7 a. ________ × 70 = 560000	7 b. 90 × ________ = 360000
8 a. 1000 × ________ = 400000	8 b. 60 × ________ = 120000
9 a. 80 × ________ = 8000	9 b. ________ × 40 = 320000
10 a. ________ × 100 = 500000	10 b. ________ × 90 = 7200

VIII: We know that 1 foot = 12 inches. In the foot scale that we use during daily study has 12 marks indicating scaling of 12 inches. What fraction of a foot is equal to 4 inches?

IX: (4 + 4 + 4 + …… 2000 times) = 8 X ____________;

X: Find a suitable number sentence for calculating number of cards shaded in the following grid.

XI: Examine your Patience..

Achiever S

Q1 Write the numerals by separating commas as per Indian and International system of numeration. (2x1=2)

Number	Indian system	International System
684384082		
567401945		

Q2 Write the following in expanded form. (4x0.5=2)

Number	Expanded form
800348301	
40123	
43567483	
906845	

Q3 Write the place value of the underlined digits. (4x1=4)

Number	Place value	Number	Place value
2450687		85006914	
17600382		438447	
630347295		49847294	
406927143		20347304	

Q4 Write the period of the underlined digit as per Indian and international system. (2x1=2)

Number	Indian system	International system
60710009		
128973640		

Q5 Find the product of the place values of two 4s in 56,94,741. (1x1=1)

Q 6. Sum total of which two consecutive multiples of 5 is equal to 40?

Q 7. Sum total of three consecutive even numbers after 12 will be ______________.

Q 8. How many vertives are there in a pentagon?

Q 9. What will be remainder if we divide four digit smallest number by 3?

Achiever T

1: Romanika was walking along with John and Cristoffy. John was on the left hand side of Cristoffi. Romanika was at the first position from left hand side of the image. Who was there walking in the middle?

2: An apple = a ten, a mango = 100 and a banana = 1; what will be the value equivalent to 32 bananas, 37 apples and 76 mangoes? Write the value in both expanded form as well as in standard form.

3: What least number should be added to four digit smallest number to make the value divisible by 3?

4: (31 + 31 + 31 + 31 ….. 1,000 times) + (69 + 69 + ….. 1000 times) = ______________

Achiever U

1. 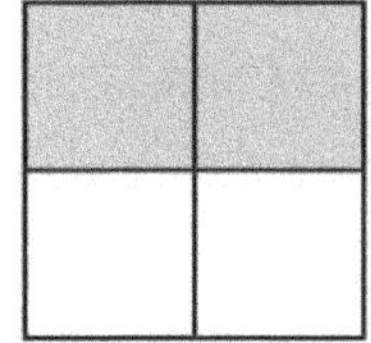 $\dfrac{1}{2}$ $\dfrac{2}{3}$ $\left(\dfrac{2}{4}\right)$ $\dfrac{1}{4}$

6. 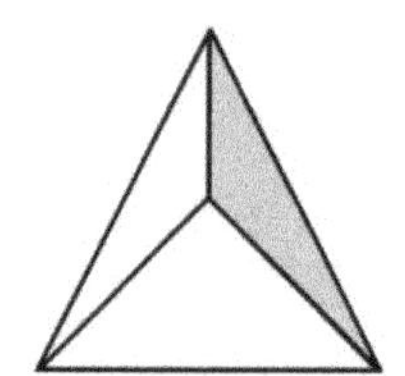 $\dfrac{1}{2}$ $\dfrac{3}{3}$ $\dfrac{1}{3}$ $\dfrac{2}{3}$

2. 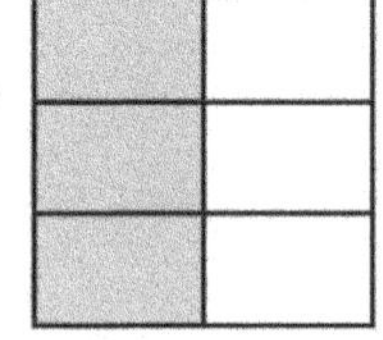 $\dfrac{3}{3}$ $\dfrac{4}{6}$ $\dfrac{2}{3}$ $\dfrac{3}{6}$

7. 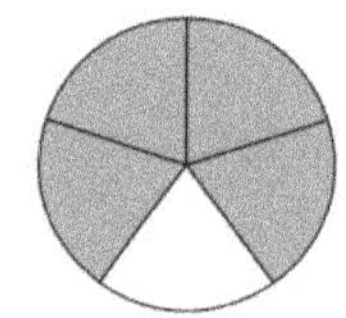 $\dfrac{3}{4}$ $\dfrac{4}{5}$ $\dfrac{1}{4}$ $\dfrac{1}{5}$

3. 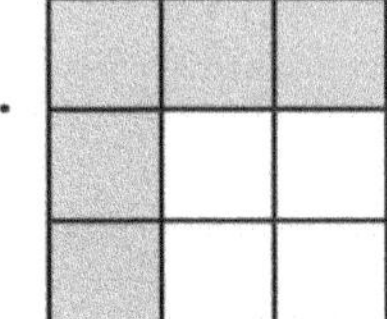 $\dfrac{2}{9}$ $\dfrac{5}{9}$ $\dfrac{4}{9}$ $\dfrac{6}{9}$

8. 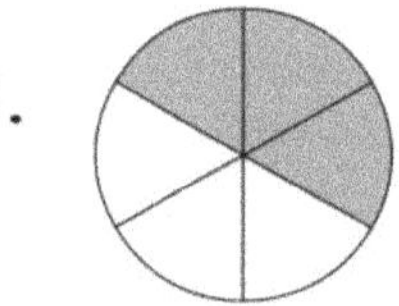 $\dfrac{1}{3}$ $\dfrac{4}{6}$ $\dfrac{3}{6}$ $\dfrac{1}{2}$

4. 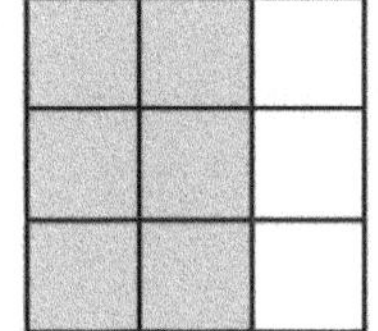 $\dfrac{3}{9}$ $\dfrac{7}{9}$ $\dfrac{6}{9}$ $\dfrac{5}{9}$

9. 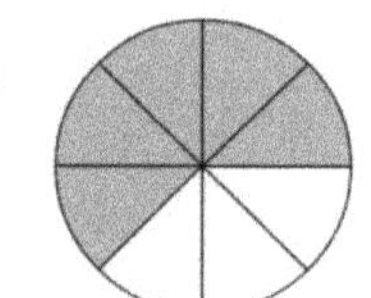 $\dfrac{1}{8}$ $\dfrac{5}{8}$ $\dfrac{1}{3}$ $\dfrac{3}{8}$

5. 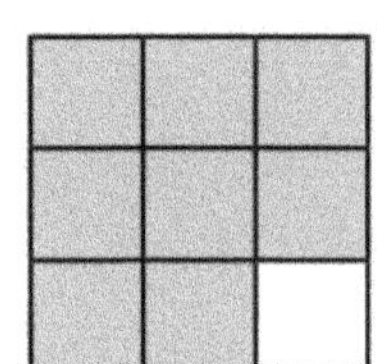 $\dfrac{8}{9}$ $\dfrac{5}{9}$ $\dfrac{1}{9}$ $\dfrac{4}{9}$

10. 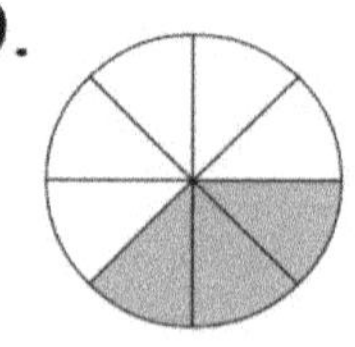 $\dfrac{5}{8}$ $\dfrac{3}{5}$ $\dfrac{3}{8}$ $\dfrac{3}{10}$

kk

6. What will be the value of half of the half of 72?

7. One fifth of a number is equal to five digit smallest number. Find the number which is three times bigger than the given number.

8: Free Time …

987 X 9	897 X 8	796 X 7
699 X 5	589 X 6	499 X 5
789 X 4	976 X 9	857 X 6
968 X 7	899 X 9	799 X 8

3)100	5)451	7)534	8)490
4)234	7)239	6)463	6)478
4)365	4)90	6)129	8)187
3)58	9)582	9)742	5)462
5)344	8)679	2)195	9)508

9: Aid Box –

① Write the equivalent fraction.

$$\frac{1}{3} = \frac{\square}{\square}$$

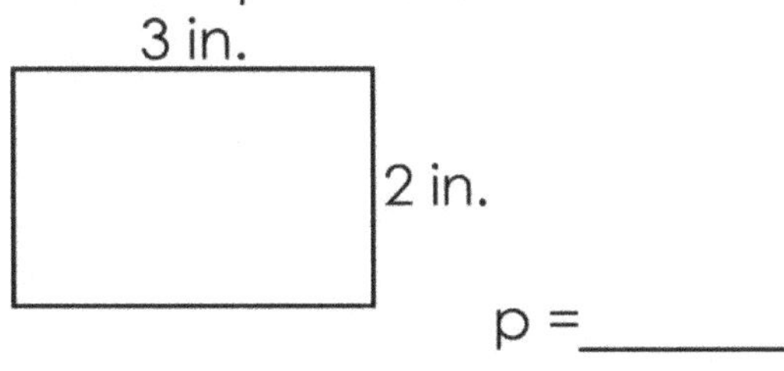

② Find the perimeter.

3 in.

2 in.

p = _______

③ Shade in the rectangles.

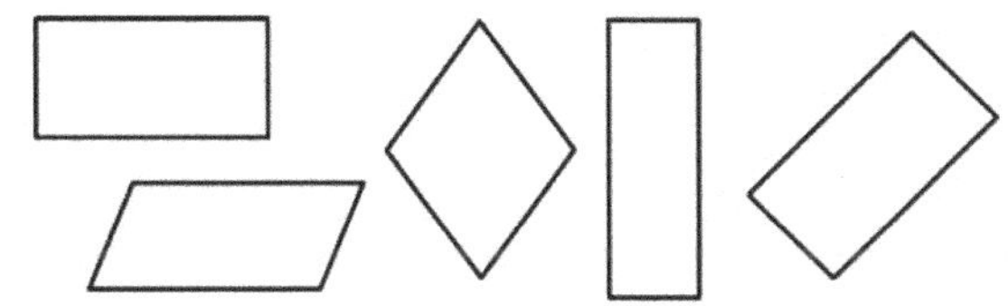

④ Sam has 15 apples. He places an equal number of apples on 3 plates. How many apples does he put on each plate? Draw a model to show your work.

⑤ Find the area.

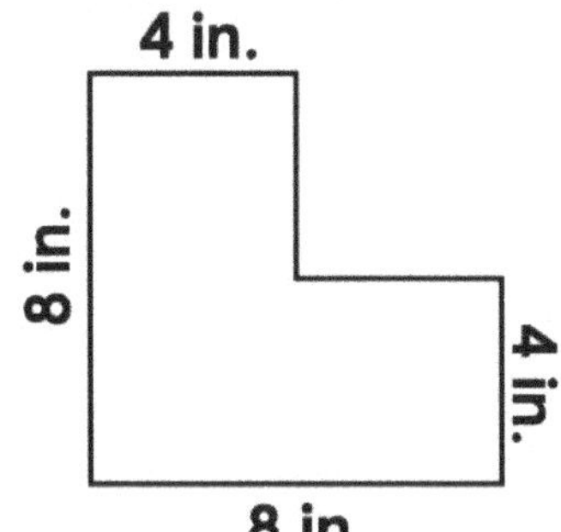

10: Aid Box –

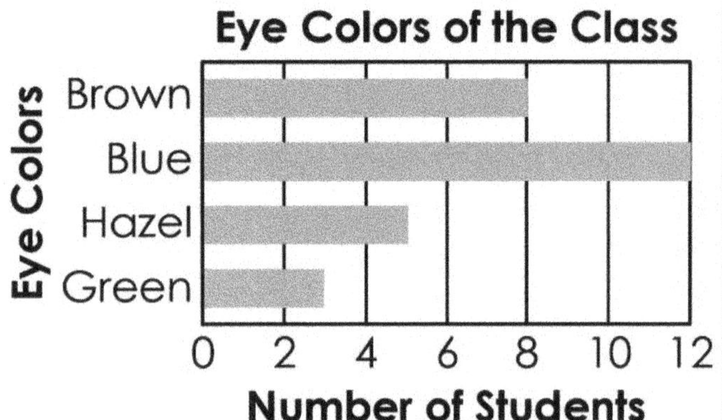

① How many students have hazel eyes?

② How many more students have blue eyes than brown?

③ How many fewer students have green eyes than brown?

④ Ally has 7 grapes. She eats 2. Then she gives 3 away. How many grapes does she have left?

$$7 - 2 = \underline{\quad\quad}$$

$$5 - 3 = \underline{\quad\quad}$$

$$g = \underline{\quad\quad}$$

She has _______ grapes left.

⑤ Compare the fractions.

$$\frac{1}{2} \bigcirc \frac{1}{4}$$

11: Complete the following....

A: (7 X 5) + (6 X 9) = _______;

B: 3 X 9 + 7 X 7 = _________;

C: 2 X 6 + 6 X 6 + 7 X 6 = _________;

D: 8 X 9 + 6 X 4 + 4 X 3 = _________;

×	0	1	2	3	4	5	6	7	8	9	10
0	0	0	0	0	0	0	0	0	0	0	0
1	0	1	2	3	4	5	6	7	8	9	10
2	0	2	4	6	8	10	12	14	16	18	20
3	0	3	6	9	12	15	18	21	24	27	30
4	0	4	8	12	16	20	24	28	32	36	40
5	0	5	10	15	20	25	30	35	40	45	50
6	0	6	12	18	24	30	36	42	48	54	60
7	0	7	14	21	28	35	42	49	56	63	70
8	0	8	16	24	32	40	48	56	64	72	80
9	0	9	18	27	36	45	54	63	72	81	90
10	0	10	20	30	40	50	60	70	80	90	100

Model Paper IV

1. Which of the following shows correct descending order?

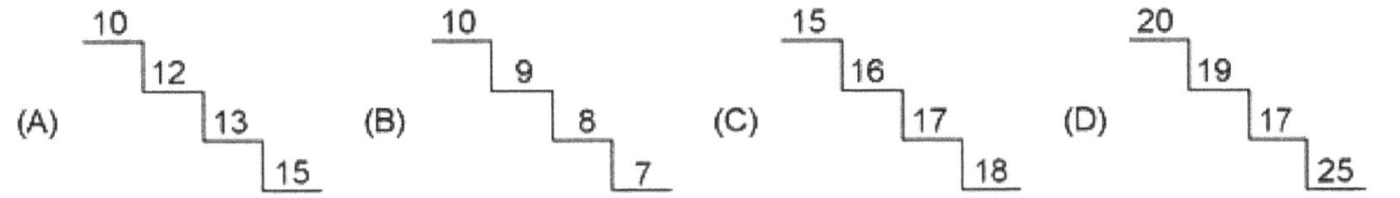

(A) 10, 12, 13, 15   (B) 10, 9, 8, 7   (C) 15, 16, 17, 18   (D) 20, 19, 17, 25

2. Latika, Monika and Sonika are sitting in a row. Latika is sitting between Monika and Sonika. Which of the following is the correct order?

(A)

Latika	Sonika	Monika

(B)

Latika	Monika	Sonika

(C)

Sonika	Latika	Monika

(D)

Sonika	Monika	Latika

3. The  can jump two steps at a time. If it is at 5th step, where will it be after 2 jumps?

(A) 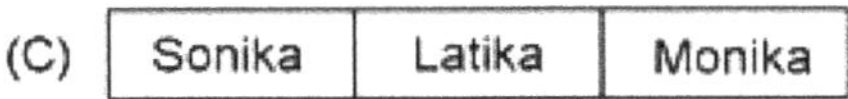

(B)

(C)   (D)

4. Four friends are celebrating their birthdays. The candles on cake shows their ages. Who is the eldest?

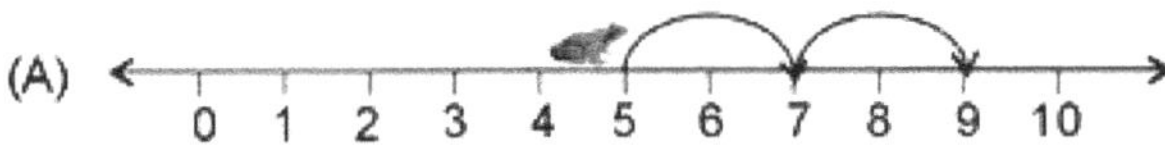

(A) Ankit   (B) Parul   (C) Ruchi   (D) Anu

5. Given two baskets shows the number of apples.

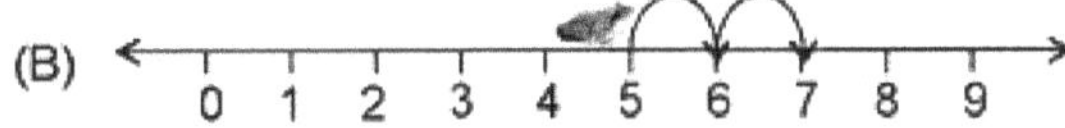

Yellow basket   Red basket

Which is correct statement?
(A) Yellow basket has <u>more</u> apples than red basket.
(B) Red basket has <u>more</u> apples than yellow basket.
(C) Both red and yellow baskets have equal apples.
(D) Red basket has <u>less</u> apples than yellow basket.

6. Which number in the following number pattern is just before 30?

22	24	26	28	30

(A) 26   (B) 28   (C) 24   (D) 22

Model Paper V

1. Find L.C.M. of following numbers

12, 24, 48, 108

(A) 504   (B) 432   (C) 405   (D) 440   (E) None of these.

2. Gita has 558 flags to pack into boxes. Each box will hold 62 flags. How many boxes will Gita need to hold all the flags ?

(A) 34,596   (B) 0.9   (C) 9   (D) 620   (E) None of these.

3. You would need to know the perimeter of something if you were--
(A) Buying a box big enough to hold a clock
(B) Buying enough tiles to cover the floor of a room
(C) Buying enough wood to make a frame for a picture
(D) Buying a tablecloth big enough to cover a table
(E) None of these.

4.

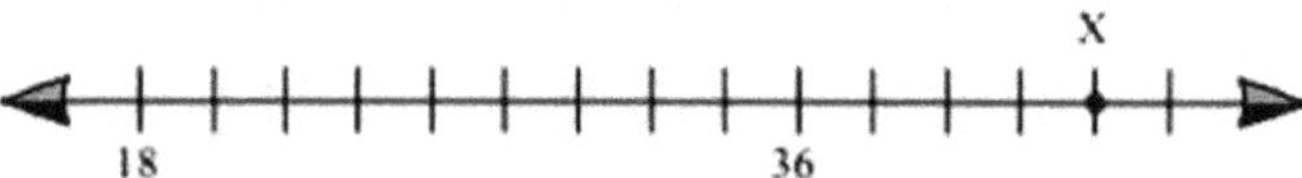

Which best describes the location of point X ?

(A) 58   (B) 40   (C) 44   (D) 54   (E) None of these.

5. What is the area of a rectangle that measures 5 meters wide and 6 meters long ?

(A) 11 m^2 (B) 22 m^2 (C) 30 m^2 (D) 16 m^2 (E) None of these.

6. If n represents a number, which of these means the same as the expression $n + 6$?

(A) Six more than a number   (B) Six divided by a number
(C) Six less than a number   (D) Six times a number   (E) None of these.

7. Which can be solved by using the open sentence $K + 10 = $?
(A) Mohan did 10 times as many push-ups as Kiran. If K is the number of push-ups Kiran did, how many push-ups did Mohan do ?
(B) Sharon did 10 more sit-ups than Kevin. If K is the number of sit-ups Kevin did, how many sit-ups did Sharon do ?
(C) John ran 10 fewer meters than Kiran. If K is the number of meters Kiran ran, how many meters did John run ?
(D) Kavita takes 10 minutes to run each lap around the gymnasium. If K is the number of laps Kavita ran, how long did she run ?
(E) None of these.

8. **Some letters are given which are numbered 1, 2, 3, 4 and 5. Find that combination of numbers so that letters arranged accordingly form a meaningful word.**

E L P T A

1 2 3 4 5

    (A) 5, 2, 3, 4, 1   (B) 5, 2, 3, 1, 4   (C) 3, 1, 4, 5, 2   (D) 5, 4, 1, 2, 3

9. **Find a figure from the options which completes the Fig. (X).**

(A) 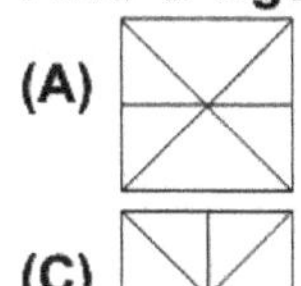   (B) 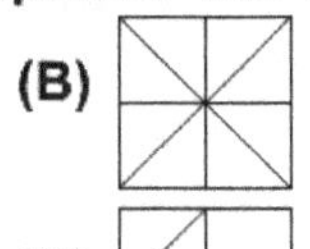

(C)    (D)

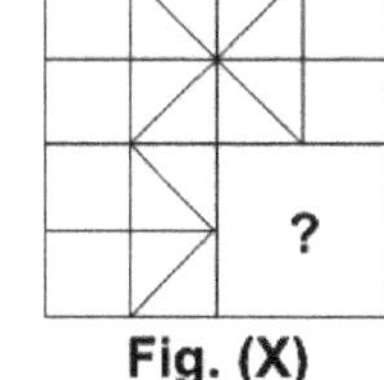

Fig. (X)

10. **Standing on a platform, Amit told Sonia that Delhi was more than 10 km but less than 15 km from there. Sonia knew that it was more than 12 km but less than 14 km. If both of them were correct, which of the following could be the distance of Delhi from there?**

    (A) 11 km   (B) 12 km   (C) 13 km   (D) 15 km

11. **In the following series one term is wrong. Find the wrong term.**

2, 18, 4, 20, 8, 22, 16, 25, 32, 26

    (A) 18   (B) 16   (C) 25   (D) 32

12. **How many unit cubes are there in the given figure?**

    (A) 38

    (B) 48

    (C) 51

    (D) 46

13. **The given question consists of figures (i), (ii), (iii) and (iv). There is a definite relationship between figures (i) and (ii). Establish a similar relationship between figures (iii) and (iv) by selecting a suitable figure from the options that would replace (?) in figure (iv).**

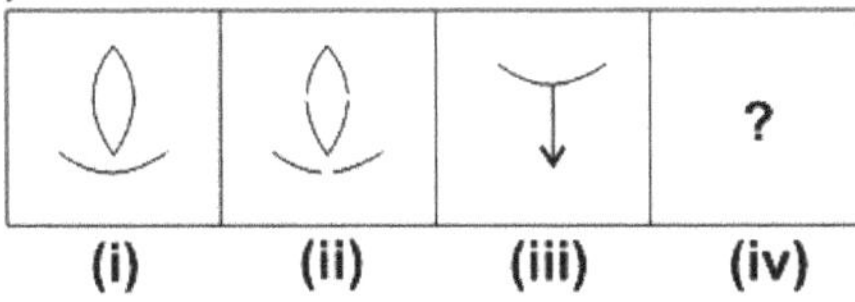

    (i)   (ii)   (iii)   (iv)

(A) 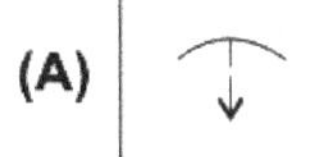   (B) 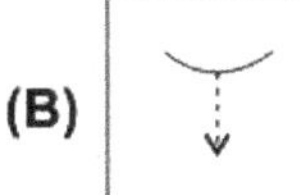   (C) 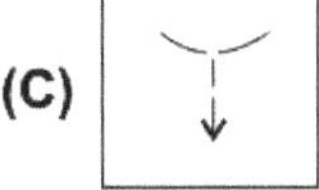   (D) 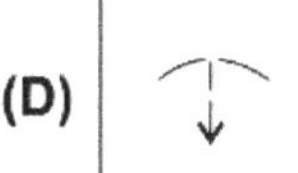

Model Paper VI

1. A rat runs 20 m towards East and turns to right, runs 10 m and turns to right, runs 9 m and again turns to left, runs 5 m and turns to left, runs 12 m and finally turns to left and runs 6 m. Now which direction is the rat facing?

   (A) East   (B) West   (C) North   (D) South

2. Choose the odd numeral pair/group in the given question :

   (A) 2 – 8   (B) 3 – 27   (C) 4 – 32   (D) 5 – 125

3. The given question contains four problem figures marked 1, 2, 3 and 4. Select a figure from amongst the options which will continue the same series as given in the Problem figures.

   (A)   (B)   (C)   (D)

4. What comes next in the given pattern ?

   10, 19, 40, 77, 158, __?__

   (A) 311   (B) 307   (C) 301   (D) 299

5. Count the number of cubes in the given figure.

   (A) 23

   (B) 24

   (C) 25

   (D) None of these

6. Two positions of a dice are given. When 2 is at the top, which of the following numbers could be at the bottom?

   (A) 1   (B) 2

   (C) 3   (D) 4

7. If 7 * 1 = 64; 3 * 9 = 144. What is the value of 5 * 6 ?

   (A) 22   (B) 55   (C) 66   (D) 121

8. 20 friends meet at a marriage reception of their common friend. Everyone of 20 friends shook hands with each other only once. Find the number of handshakes.

   (A) 400   (B) 380   (C) 40   (D) 190

9. Which of the given options will come next in the given series ?

   ZUA, XOC, VIE, TCG, __?__

   (A) RAI   (B) SAG   (C) RAG   (D) RWI

10. Find the sum ttal of first five consecutive even numbers after 10.

11. What least number should be subtracted from 10,000 to make the value exactly divisible by 3?

12. Think and write ..

Find missing numbers.

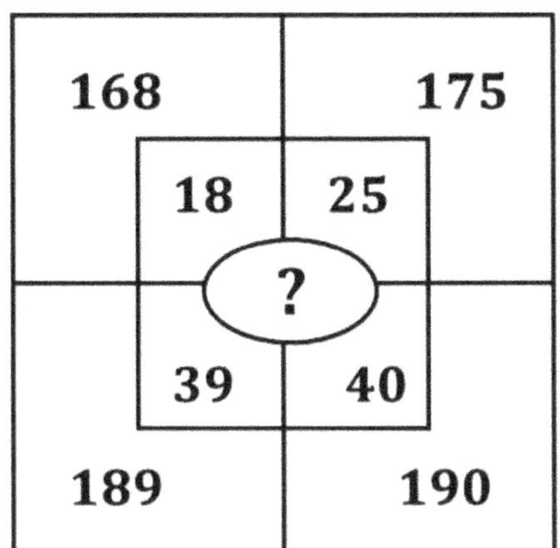

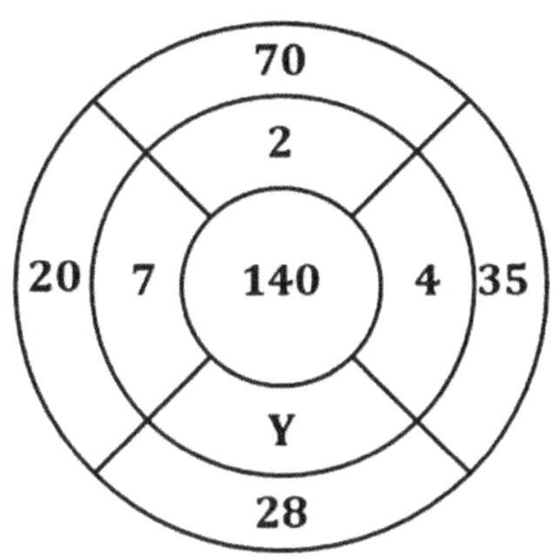

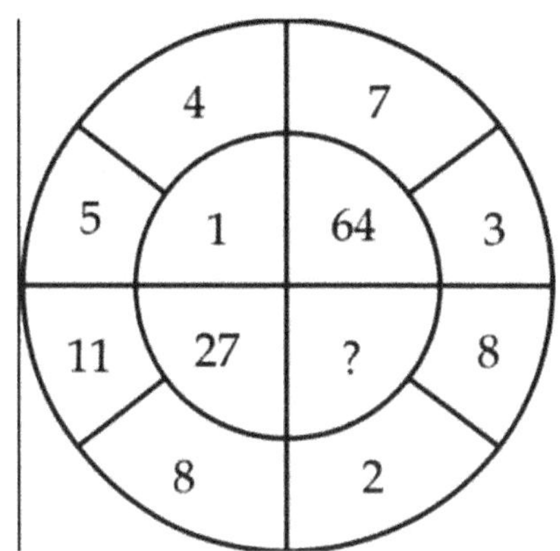

Find outer boundary of the following:

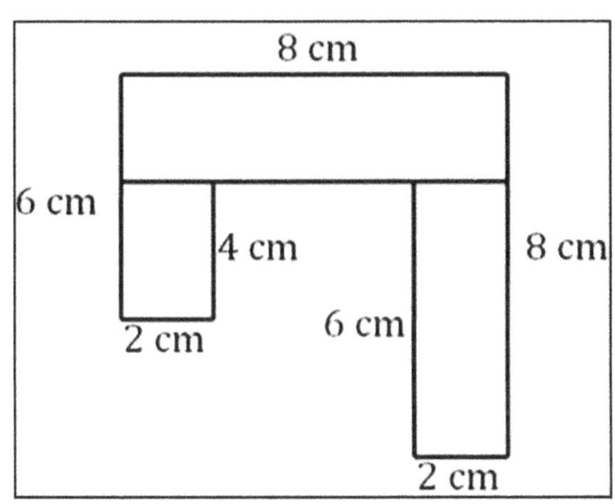

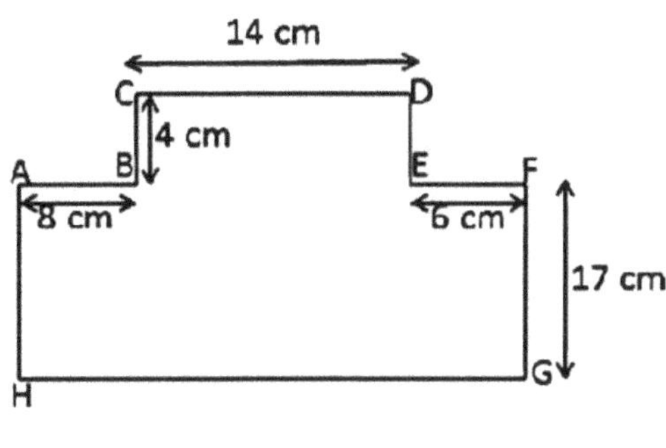

13. Find the following.

 +  = 74 kg,  +  + = 84 kg

 =

____

Model Paper VII

Match the columns:

1. 1:00 p.m to 3:00 p.m.	**a)** 40 minutes
2. 6:30 a.m. to 7:45 a.m.	**b)** 1 hour and 20 minutes
3. 12:30 p.m. to 1:10 p.m.	**c)** 23 hours and 35 minutes
4. 2:35 p.m. to 6:20 p.m.	**d)** 2 hours
5. 11:45 p.m. to 1:05 a.m.	**e)** 12 hours and 45 minutes
6. 4:50 a.m. to 9:20 a.m.	**f)** 1 hour and 15 minutes
7. 8:20 a.m. to 2:35 p.m.	**g)** 6 hours and 15 minutes
8. 3:05 p.m. to 9:25 p.m.	**h)** 4 hours and 30 minutes
9. 9:15 p.m. to 8:50 p.m.	**i)** 3 hours and 45 minutes
10. 5:10 a.m. to 5:55 p.m.	**j)** 6 hours and 20 minutes

11: Write a suitable number sentence for counting the articles present in the grid.

12: An apple = ______________ g.

13: Solve the following.

14: Complete the following:

(5 + 5 + ….100 times) + (95 + 95 + …. 100 times) = __________.

21 hundreds + 21 tens + 54 ones + 18 hundreds = __________.

15: Solve:

16: Following figure shows how balls balance cans in a beam balance. 64 balls = _______ cans.

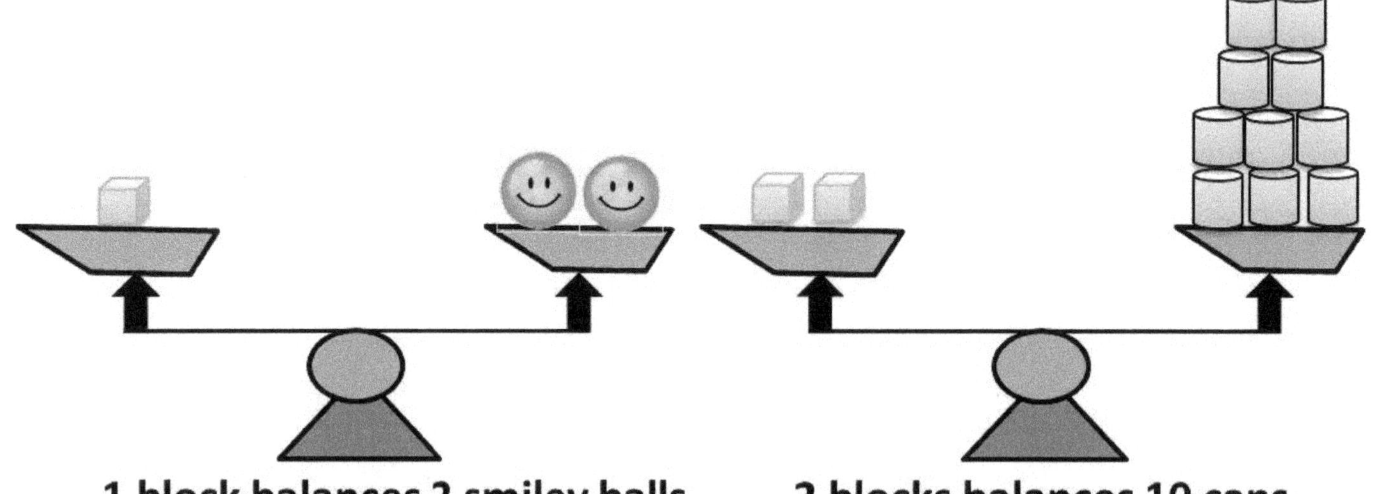

17: Calculate:

$$\square + 30g = \square \quad \square - \bigcirc = 60g$$

$$7\,\square,\ 7\,\square \text{ and } 7\,\bigcirc = 4{,}200\ g$$

$$\bigcirc = \underline{\qquad}\ g$$

18: Find the values:

A  = _______ ml

B  = _______ ml

C  = _______ ml

D 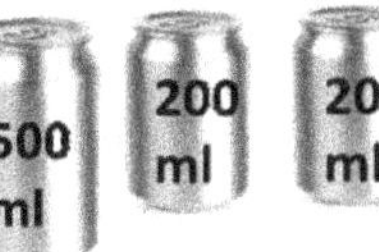 = _______ ml

E  = _______ ml

I: (A + B + C)X2 − E = _______.   II: (D + B + A)X2 − E = _______.

III: E = _______. [Options 2A / 2B/ 2C/ 2D ;

19: 20 km 16 m + 32 km 160 m = _______________.

20: Find the value.

$$\text{cylinder} + \text{cube} = 180\ g$$

$$\text{pentagon} + \text{cylinder} + \text{cube} = 230\ g$$

$$\text{pentagon} + \text{pentagon} + \text{cylinder} + \text{cube} = \underline{\quad\quad}$$

21. 21 hundreds + 43 tens + 65 hundreds + 65 ones = _______________.

22. The given figure shows two identical rectangles, each measuring 8 cm by 4 cm, overlapping one another. The shaded area is $\frac{1}{4}$ the area of each rectangle. Find the area of the unshaded part of the figure.

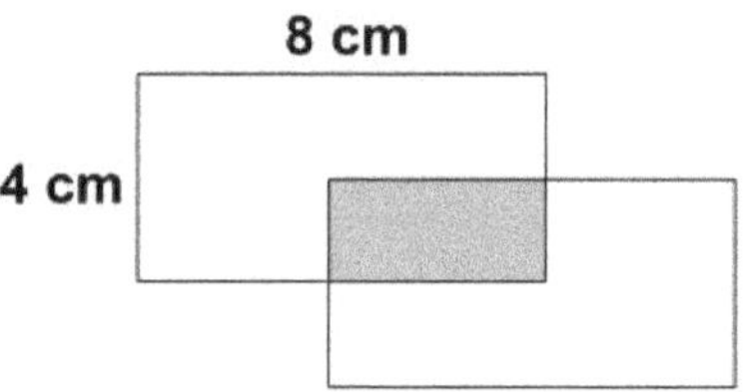

(A) 24 cm²   (B) 48 cm²   (C) 56 cm²   (D) 64 cm²

23. How many more triangles must be shaded so that half of the given figure is shaded?
(A) 3
(B) 4
(C) 5
(D) 6

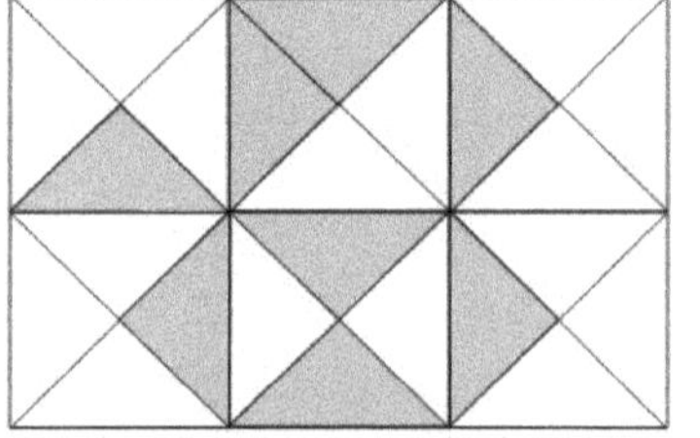

24. What is two hundred four thousand, four hundred and forty one in numerals ?
(A) 24441   (B) 24401   (C) 204441   (D) 240441

25. How many right angles does the second hand of a clock travel through from 6:15 p.m. to 6:18 p.m. ?
(A) 4   (B) 8   (C) 12   (D) 16

26. The diagram shows a simplified model of a trolley that is used in supermarkets. How many vertical lines would there be in five such trolleys ?

(A) 70

(B) 16

(C) 14

(D) 80

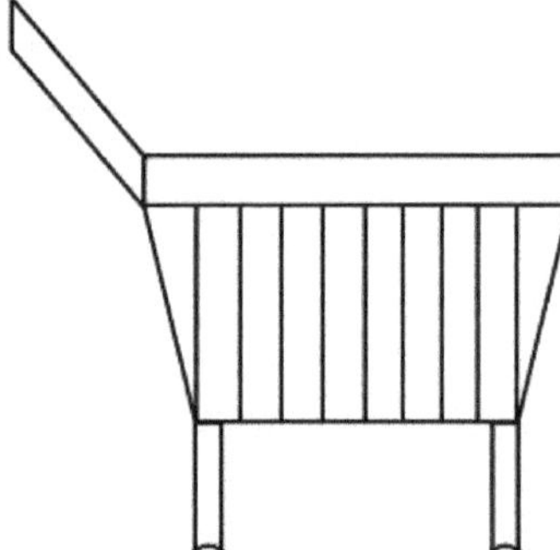

27. Rectangles A, B and C are identical. Find the perimeter of the figure.

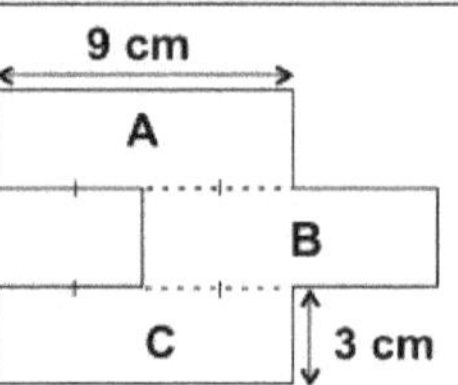

(A) 36 cm   (B) 45 cm

(C) 54 cm   (D) 63 cm

28. Each of the letters A and B given below represents a specific digit.

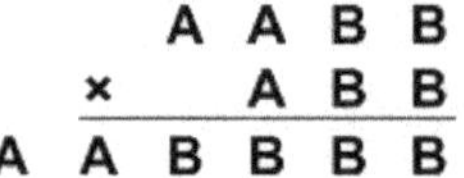

```
    A A B B
×     A B B
A A B B B B
```

Which one of the following digits does A represent?
(A) 1   (B) 2   (C) 3   (D) 0

22. A table costs ₹ 560. What will be the cost of 3 such tables?

    A. ₹ 1,680   B. ₹ 1,240   C. ₹ 960   D. ₹ 1,560

23. Jyoti wants to distribute 875 marbles equally in 7 groups. How many marbles are there in each group?

    A. 125   B. 175   C. 126   D. 176

24. Piyush is 167 cm tall. His sister is 29 cm shorter than Piyush. What is the total height of Piyush and his sister?

    A. 1 m 38 cm   B. 1 m 96 cm   C. 3 m 5 cm   D. 3 m 50 cm

25. Ravi bought 7 cans of paint and used 4 cans. What fraction of the paint did he use?

    A. 1/7   B. 4/7   C. 3/7   D. 6/7

26. In the year 2009, there were 198 working school days. How many days were holidays?

    A. 165   B. 167   C. 200   D. 205

27. Akshat collected 352 old coins. His friend collected 212 old coins. How many old coins do they both collected altogether?

    A. 564   B. 566   C. 664   D. 666

28. 46 children from class III contributed ₹ 25 each for some relief fund. How much money did the class contribute in all?

    A. ₹ 910   B. ₹ 920   C. ₹ 1,050   D. ₹ 1,150

29. A teacher wants to stand 50 children in rows of 7 each. How many rows did they make? How many children were left?

    A. 6, 3   B. 8, 2   C. 7, 1   D. 9, 1

30. Rohan has

    One-third of the balloons burst. How many balloons burst?

    A. 1   B. 2   C. 3   D. 4